How to Win the Job Interview

Success in English Interview for Cabin Crew

항공 승무원을 위한 **성공 영어 인터뷰**

면접에서
승리하는
방법

 Preface

「Success in English Interview for Cabin Crew」 is a handy book for all prospective job seeking second language students to gain practical English interview skills. This is the second book of 「English Interview for Cabin Crew」, which was published in August of 2017. Success in English Interview for Cabin Crew will include additional interview questions and responses as well as important processes of writing a resume and a cover letter for prospective job seeking students. The content of this book will include interview topics such as creating a resume, a cover letter, and answering common and difficult interview questions as well as behavioral and scenario interview questions. This book can be used by all students, especially for second language learners in various majors, including but not limited to, airline service, tourism, business administration, and English. The main goal of this book is to help English language learners to communicate meaningfully and confidently in English during their job interviews, but to also help them obtain job interviews by creating a strong resume and a cover letter.

Chapter organization consists of seven parts:

<u>Goals</u> help students to focus on the main learning they will do in each chapter.

<u>Grammar Points</u> provide a glimpse into the chapter's key grammar points.

<u>Key Vocabulary</u> highlights key and pertinent words that are covered in each chapter. Reviewing the key vocabulary will help students understand each chapter different interview questions and responses.

Interview Tips provide important job interview techniques and skills to help students to be prepared and to interview effectively when it is time for the real job interviews.

Interview Questions & Sample Responses outline interview questions and sample responses for each chapter.

Key Words & Expressions present some of the language patterns and expressions used in different topics for each chapter.

Communicative Activities provide purposeful opportunities for students to practice the important grammar structures meaningfully and appropriately. The activities will also allow students to develop all four aspects of language skills: listening, speaking, reading, and writing.

이제시카선규

머리말

『항공 승무원을 위한 성공 영어 인터뷰』는 실용 영어 인터뷰 기술을 습득하기 위한 것으로 취업을 준비하는 모든 학생에게 이상적인 교재입니다. 이 교재는 2017년 8월에 출판된 『항공 승무원을 위한 영어 인터뷰』의 두 번째 교재입니다. 본서는 예비 취업 학생을 위한 이력서 및 커버 레터 (cover letter) 작성의 중요한 프로세스를 포함되어 있습니다. 본서의 내용에는 이력서 작성법, 커버 레터 작성법, 공통적이고 어려운 면접 질문 및 대응법 그리고 시나리오, 실제 상황극, 인터뷰 질문에 대한 답변과 같은 내용이 포함됩니다. 본서는 모든 학생 특히 항공서비스, 관광학, 경영학, 영어를 포함한 다양한 전공에서 영어를 학습하는 학생들에게 유용합니다. 이 교재의 주요 목표 중 하나는 취업 면접을 준비하는 학생들이 의미있고 자신있게 영어로 의사소통 할 수 있도록 도와주며, 나아가 강력한 이력서와 커버 레터를 작성하여 면접을 준비할 수 있도록 돕습니다.

챕터 구성은 일곱개 영역으로 구성되어 있습니다.

<u>목표</u>는 학생들이 각 장에서 할 수 있는 주요 학습에 초점을 맞출 수 있도록 도와줍니다.

<u>핵심 문법</u> 섹션에서는 각 장의 핵심 문법 포인트를 제시합니다.

<u>주요 어휘에서는</u> 각 장에서 다루는 핵심 단어와 관련 단어를 강조합니다. 주요 어휘를 검토하면 학생들이 각 장의 여러 면접 질문과 답변을 이해하는 데 도움이 됩니다.

<u>인터뷰 팁</u>은 중요한 인터뷰 방법과 기술을 제공하여 학생들이 실제 취업 면접을 준비 할 때 효과적으로 인터뷰 할 수 있도록 도와줍니다.

<u>인터뷰 질문 및 응답샘플</u>에서는 인터뷰 질문 및 각 장의 샘플 답변을 간략하게 요약합니다.

<u>핵심 단어 및 표현</u> 섹션에서는 각 장마다 서로 다른 주제로 사용되는 언어 패턴과 표현의 일부를 제시합니다.

<u>의사소통 활동</u> 에서는 학생들이 의미 있고 적절하게 중요한 문법 구조를 연습할 수 있는 기회를 제공합니다. 이 실전 활동을 통해 학생들은 듣기, 말하기, 읽기 및 쓰기의 네가지 언어 능력을 개발할 수 있습니다.

이제시카선규

Contents

Success in English Interview for Cabin Crew: How to Win the Job Interview

항공 승무원을 위한 성공 영어 인터뷰:
면접에서 승리하는 방법

Chapter 01

Guidelines for Job Interview:
Basic Interview Skills

면접을 위한 지침:
기본 인터뷰 기술

Chapter 01

Guidelines for Job Interview: Basic Interview Skills
면접을 위한 지침: 기본 인터뷰 기술

What are the basic guidelines for a successful job interview?
성공적인 면접을 위한 기본 지침은 무엇인가?

It is possible that some people get hired for the career they want as a result of luck and good fortune. It may also be that those fortunate people aced the job interview, which made it possible for them to obtain the career they desired. However, most people know that in order to have a successful job interview, they need to invest time to improve their interview skills. Fortunately, interview skills can be learned and the more you practice, interview tactics can be improved. Even the most qualified and skilled job applicants spend time preparing for their job interviews. Investing extra time preparing for the interview can make the interview process much more smooth and less stressful. Here are the basic guidelines when preparing for a successful job interview:

어떤 사람들은 기회가 좋아서 그들이 원하는 직업으로 취업 될 수도 있다. 또한 그러한 사람들이 취업 면접을 통해 좋은 성적으로 자신이 원하는 직업을 얻을 수 있게 되었을 수도 있다. 그러나 대부분의 사람들은 성공적인 면접을 하기 위해서 인터뷰 기술을 향상시키는 데 시간을 투자해야 한다는 것을 알아야 한다. 다행스럽게도 인터뷰 기술을 습득하고 연습 할 수록 인터뷰 전략이 개선 될 수 있다. 심지어 가장 능력있고 숙련된 구직자들도 면접을 준비 하는 데 시간을 보낸다. 인터뷰 준비를 위한 추가 시간을 투자하면 면접 과정을 훨씬 더 유연하게 하고, 스트레스를 적게 받는다. 성공적인 취업 면접을 준비 할 때 필요한 기본 지침은 다음과 같다.

Be Prepared and Practice
준비하고 연습하라

Do your homework and do research about the company and the industry you are interested in applying. Visit the company's website and read any current news about the company. Ask relevant people for any additional information. Then develop a short list of questions you can ask during the interview. Similarly, prepare responses to common questions often asked at a job interview.

숙제를 하고 회사 및 업계에 대한 조사를 하라. 회사 웹 사이트를 방문하여 회사에 관한 최신 뉴스를 읽어라. 관련된 사람들에게 추가 정보를 요청한다. 그런 다음 면접을 하면서 질문할 수 있는 짧은 목록을 작성하라. 마찬가지로 취업 면접에서 자주 제기되는 일반적인 질문에 대한 답변을 준비한다.

Dress Professionally
전문적인 복장을 갖춰라

Research the typical dress code for that particular business and dress accordingly. Some companies have dress code requirements, so always adhere to the requirements. It is better to dress up than down. Don't forget to review and do your hair and makeup appropriately as well. The interviewers always notice everything about you. This includes your attire, hair-style, and makeup.

특정 비즈니스에 맞는 전형적인 복장을 알고 그에따른 복장을 착용한다. 일부 회사는 드레스 코드 요구 사항을 가지고 있으므로 항상 요구 사항을 준수해야 한다. 가능하면 옷을 더 잘 입는 것이 낫다. 헤어스타일과 메이크업을 적절하게 검토하고 수행하는 것을 잊지 마라. 면접관은 항상 당신에 관한 모든 것을 관찰하고 있다. 여기에는 복장, 헤어스타일 및 메이크업이 포함된다.

Arrive on Time
정각에 도착하라

This means arriving 15 to 30 minutes prior to the appointment time. If necessary, visit the interview location ahead of time. Calculate the traffic time and make a plan to arrive early for the interview.

이것은 약속 시간 15분 ~ 30분 전에 도착해야 한다는 것을 의미한다. 필요한 경우 미리 인터뷰 장소를 방문하라. 교통 시간을 계산하고 인터뷰를 위해 일찍 도착할 계획을 세워라.

Practice Good Nonverbal Communication
좋은 비언어적 의사소통을 실천하라

When meeting your interviewers, you want to make an effective first impression. Demonstrate good posture and make good eye contact. Your greeting should consist of a genuine smile, good eye contact, and a firm handshake if appropriate. Providing a genuine smile during an interview can provide a positive impression.

면접관을 만날 때, 효과적인 첫인상을 만들어야 한다. 좋은 자세를 보여주고 상대방의 눈을 맞추도록 하라. 당신의 인사말은 진정한 미소, 좋은 시선, 적절한 악수로 구성되어야 한다. 인터뷰 중 진정한 미소를 지으면 긍정적인 인상을 줄 수 있다.

Interview With Confidence
자신감 있게 면접하라

You have been selected for an interview, which indicates that you have the ability/qualification for the job. Therefore, demonstrate what you know with confidence. The interviewers will have more credibility in your ability when you interview with confidence.

당신은 면접을 위해 선발되었으므로, 해당 직무에 대한 능력/자격이 있음을 알 수 있다. 따라서 자신감을 가지고 자신이 아는 것을 보여 주어야 한다. 자신감 있게 인터뷰 할 때 자신의 능력에 면접관은 더 많은 신뢰감을 갖게 된다.

Use Polite Language
정중한 언어를 사용하라

Always use professional and polite language during the job interview. The interview process is a professional meeting place. Regardless of how comfortable the interviewers make you feel, do not let your guard down. Always be professional and use polite language.

취업 면접에서는 항상 전문적이고 정중한 언어를 사용하라. 면접 과정은 전문적인 만남의 장소이다. 면접관이 얼마나 편안하게 느끼는지에 관계없이, 편하게 생각하면 안 된다. 항상 전문적이며 정중한 언어를 사용하라.

Answer the Interview Questions
인터뷰 질문에 답하라

When interviewers ask for an example of a time when you did something, use that opportunity to illustrate your ability and skills. The interviewers are trying to elicit your problem-solving skills and your past behaviors.

면접관들이 여러분이 무엇을 했을 때 사례를 요구하면, 그 기회를 이용하여 여러분의 능력과 기술을 설명하도록 하라. 면접관은 문제해결 능력과 과거 행동을 끌어내기 위해 질문하고 있다.

Ask Questions During Interview
면접에서 질문하라

If given an opportunity to ask questions during or at the end of the interview, please take advantage of it to ask questions. Asking questions demonstrates that you have an interest in the company.

인터뷰 도중 또는 인터뷰가 끝날 때 질문 할 수 있는 기회가 주어지면 질문을 활용하라. 질문을 하는 것은 당신이 회사에 관심이 있음을 보여준다.

The Basic Hiring Requirements for Cabin Crew
항공 승무원을 위한 기본 채용 요건

Getting hired as a flight attendant requires a lengthy process. There are different levels of interview processes and assessment steps. However, before one can even be invited for an interview, every applicant has to fulfill basic hiring requirements.

승무원으로 고용되기 까지 많은 시간이 걸린다. 인터뷰와 평가 과정에는 여러 단계가 있다. 하지만 면접에 응시하기 전에 모든 지원자들은 기본적인 채용 기준을 충족해야 한다.

Application Screening 서류심사 → First Interview 1차 면접 → Second Interview (English Assessment) 2차 면접 (영어 면접) → Third Interview 3차 면접 → Health Fitness Test 건강체력 진단 → Final Decision Announced → 최종 합격자 발표

Each airline has its own hiring requirements. The following list provides basic hiring requirements.

각 항공사는 자체적으로 채용기준을 가지고 있다. 다음 목록은 기본적인 채용기준을 제시한다.

☑ Age (Minimum age: 18 to 21 years, depending on the airline)
연령 (최소 만 연령 18 ~ 21세, 항공사에 따라 다름)

☑ Height (Minimum 160 cm or taller, depending on the airline)
신장 (최소 160 cm 이상, 항공사에 따라 다름)

☑ Arm Reach Length (Minimum 208 cm or above-can be on tippy-toes, depending on the airline)

arm reach 길이 (최소 208 cm 이상-발가락 위에 있을 수 있다, 항공사에 따라 다름)

☑ Weight (Be proportional to your weight)
체중 (당신의 신체에 맞는 적당한 체중)

☑ Vision (Corrected Eye Sight Above 1.0)
시력 (교정시력 1.0 이상)

☑ Language Proficiency (Minimum TOEIC Score of 550 or above and HSK Requirement, depending on the airline)
언어 능력 (최소 TOEIC 550 점 이상, HSK 요구 사항, 항공사에 따라 다름)

☑ Education Level (Associate Degree or higher, depending on the airline)
교육수준 (2년제 졸업 이상, 항공사에 따라 다름)

☑ Physical Ability (Lifting medium to heavy baggage into overhead bins/pushing a 200lb service cart up and down the isle/keeping balance during the flight/working long hours/managing jet lag and etc.)
신체능력 (무거운 짐을 머리위로 올리기/90kg 의 서비스 카트 밀기/비행중에 균형 유지/장기간 근무/시차적응 관리 등)

☑ Physical Appearance (Well groomed/neat/conservative-no tattoos/no piercing except in the ears)
이미지 (건강한/근사함/단정함-문신이 없는/귀를 제외하고 피어싱 없는)

☑ Personal Qualities/Characteristics (Work well under pressure or in a team/do multitask effectively/have professional and work ethics and etc.)
인성 (팀에서의 적응능력, 다양한 일을 효과적으로 수행하는 능력, 전문성과 직업윤리 등)

Open Day vs. Assessment Day

오픈데이와 평가 날

Open Day 하고 Assessment Day 행사는 주로 외국항공사 대상으로 개최된다.

An Open Day event is an information or recruitment session that is publicly opened for all prospective applicants. Foreign airlines usually announce their Open Days approximately two months before the event date. Although anyone can go to an Open Day event, many airlines recommend that those who are participating to register online prior to the event. During this event, there will be presentations about what is like to work as a cabin crew and to live in the airline's country. All participants are recommended to wear formal business attire and bring standard documents, such as a CV/resume, passport photos, and a full-length photo. Some airlines require a photocopy of the first page of your passport and a copy of your highest education diploma in its original language. All participants have an opportunity to drop off their CVs/resumes, but only a few will be invited to an assessment day event.

오픈데이 (Open Day) 행사는 모든 예비 신청자들을 위해 정보나 채용조건을 공개적으로 제공하는 것이다. 외국항공사는 일반적으로 행사일 2개월 전부터 공개 날짜를 발표한다. 누구나 오픈데이 (Open Day) 행사에 참여할 수 있지만, 많은 항공사는 행사에 앞서 온라인으로 사람들이 등록하기를 추천한다. 이 행사 중에는 항공 승무원으로 일하고 항공사의 국가에 사는 것에 대한 프레젠테이션이 있을 것이다. 모든 참가자는 정식 비즈니스 복장을 착용하고 CV / 이력서, 여권 사진 및 전신사진과 같은 기본서류를 가져 오는 것을 권장한다. 일부 항공사들은 여권 첫 장의 사본과 당신의 모국어로 된 최종 학위 증명서 사본을 요구한다. 모든 참가자는 자신의 CV/이력서를 제출할 기회가 있지만 평가일(Assessment Day)에는 소수의 참가자만 초청된다.

An Assessment Day event provides different stages for assessors to assess candidates. The event is open to those candidates who have been invited from the Open Day event and whose applications were selected on the airline's website. The event usually starts with a presentation of the airline, followed by an arm reach test, a group exercise, an English test, and a final interview. Only successful candidates are given the invitation to move to the next state. Unsuccessful candidates will be eliminated throughout each stage. Only those candidates who made it to the final stage will be asked to come back the next day for a final interview.

(Assessment Day) 평가일에는 평가자가 응시자를 평가할 수 있는 다양한 단계를 제공한다. 행사는 오픈데이 (Open Day) 행사에서 초청된 후보자와 항공사의 웹 사이트에서 선정된 후보자에게 공개된다. 그 행사는 대개 항공사의 발표로 시작하고, 이어서 arm reach 테스트, 그룹 활동, 영어 시험, 최종 면접이 뒤따른다. 합격한 후보자만 다음 단계로 이동할 수 있는 초대장을 받는다. 합격하지 못한 지원자들은 각 단계에서 탈락할 것이다. 최종 단계로 진출한 후보자들만 다음날 최종 인터뷰를 위해 다시 응시할 것을 요청 받게 될 것이다.

👥 Warm-Up Interview Questions

Q.1 Is your name _____? Can I have your name and number, please?

당신의 이름은 _____ 입니까?

당신의 이름과 응시 번호를 알려줄 수 있을까요?

Q.2 How are you today? How are you feeling today?

오늘 기분이 어떠세요?

Q.3 Where are you from?

어느 나라 사람인가요?

Q.4 Did you have any difficulty finding this place?

이 장소를 찾는데 어려움이 있었습니까?

Q.5 Where do you currently live?

지금 사는 곳이 어디입니까?

Q.6 How do you maintain good health?

건강관리를 어떻게 하시나요?

Q.7 What is your current job?

현재 무슨 일을 하나요?

Q.8 Have you applied for _____ Airline before?

전에 _____ 항공을 신청하셨습니까?

Q.9 What do you know about our airline?

우리 항공사에 대해 무엇을 아십니까?

Q.10 Is your phone number _____? Could we call you later today for the next assessment process?

전화번호는 _____ 입니까? 다음 평가 절차를 위해 오늘 늦게 전화 할 수 있습니까?

 Let's Practice English • 영어를 연습해 보자

Activity 1: Reading/Writing/Speaking 읽기/쓰기/말하기

Visit different airlines' website homepages listed in appendix 6 and learn about their recruitment requirements and hiring processes.

부록 6 에 열거 된 다양한 항공사의 웹 사이트 홈페이지를 방문하여 모집 요건 및 채용 절차에 대해 알아보아라.

Select 3 companies that you would like to interview with and write down their key recruitment requirements. Share your information with your partner.

인터뷰를 원하는 3 개의 회사를 선택하고 주요 채용 기준을 적어라. 파트너에게 정보를 공유하라.

Activity 2: Listening/Speaking 듣기/말하기

Use the warm-up questions in chapter 1 to do small talk with your partner.
Take turns asking and answering the questions.
다음 질문을 사용하여 파트너에게 물어보고 교대로 질문하고 질문에 응답하라.

Q.1 Is your name _____? Can I have your name and number, please?

당신의 이름은 _____ 입니까?

당신의 이름과 응시 번호를 알려줄 수 있을까요?

Q.2 How are you today? How are you feeling today?

오늘 기분이 어떠세요?

Q.3 Where are you from?

어느 나라 사람인가요?

Q.4 Did you have any difficulty finding this place?

이 장소를 찾는데 어려움이 있었습니까?

Q.5 Where do you currently live?

지금 사는 곳이 어디입니까?

Q.6 How do you maintain good health?

건강관리를 어떻게 하시나요?

Q.7 What is your current job?

현재 무슨 일을 하나요?

Q.8 Have you applied for _____ Airline before?

전에 _____ 항공을 신청하셨습니까?

Q.9 What do you know about our airline?

우리 항공사에 대해 무엇을 아십니까?

Q.10 Is your phone number _____? Could we call you later today for the next assessment process?

전화번호는 _____ 입니까? 다음 평가 절차를 위해 오늘 늦게 전화 할 수 있습니까?

Success in English Interview for Cabin Crew: How to Win the Job Interview

항공 승무원을 위한 성공 영어 인터뷰:
면접에서 승리하는 방법

Chapter 02

Types of English Interviews
영어 인터뷰 유형

Chapter 02

Types of English Interviews
영어 인터뷰 유형

Essential Tactics in English Interview
영어 면접의 필수 사항

In general, job interviews can be stressful, and an airline job interview in English can be even more so if English is not the interviewee's native language. Prospective flight attendants not only have to prepare for a regular job interview process, but they also have to prepare for a job interview in foreign languages. The good news is that airline English interviews can be prepared. Studying the common airline interview questions and responses in English is one of the best ways to prepare for an English interview.

일반적으로, 취업 면접은 스트레스를 줄 수 있고, 영어가 면접지원자들의 모국어가 아니기 때문에 영어로 진행되는 항공사 면접은 훨씬 더 어려울 수 있다. 예비 승무원은 정규 면접 과정을 준비할 뿐만 아니라 외국어로 취업 면접을 준비해야 한다. 좋은 소식은 항공사 영어 인터뷰가 준비될 수 있다는 것이다. 일반적인 항공사 면접 질문과 답변을 영어로 공부하는 것은 영어 면접을 준비하는 가장 좋은 방법 중 하나이다.

Airline English interviews focus on the candidates' ability to understand interview questions and their ability to express themselves in English. Thus, the key is to review common interview questions and to practice expressing oneself in English as comfortably and confidently as one can. Interviewers often ask follow-up questions to monitor candidates' understanding of the interview questions, so it is always good to prepare follow-up questions and responses with the common interview questions.

항공사 영어 인터뷰는 지원자가 인터뷰 질문을 이해하는지, 그리고 영어로 자신을 표현할 수 있는 능력에 중점을 둔다. 따라서 핵심은 일반적인 인터뷰 질문을 검토하고 영어로 자신을 편안하고 자신있게 표현하는 연습을 하는 것이다. 면접관은 인터뷰 질문에 대한 지원자의 이해를 확인하기 위해 추가 질문을 하기 때문에, 일반 면접 질문에 대한 추가 질문과 답변을 준비하는 것이 좋다.

Good Preparation Tactics for English Interview
영어 면접을 위한 최선의 준비 자세

Prepare for common interview questions & responses (follow-up questions and responses included)

일반적인 면접 질문 및 답변을 준비하라 (추가 질문 및 답변 포함).

Provide positive responses with concrete examples

구체적인 예시를 통해 긍정적인 답변을 준비하라.

Speak comfortably and confidently

편안하고 자신있게 말하라.

Use simple, clear & polite language

간결하고 명확하며 공손한 언어를 사용하라.

Practice good eye contact and body gestures

편안한 시선처리와 비언어적 요소를 활용하라.

Types of English Interviews
영어 면접 유형

<u>One-on-One Interview</u> - An one-on-one interview takes place in person with one to three hiring representatives of the airline. The content of the interview questions will be guided by application documents, such as a resume, a cover letter, and an application as well as simple small talk conversation.

<u>1:1 면접</u> – 1:1 면접은 항공사의 면접관 1~3명을 만나게 된다. 면접 질문의 내용은 이력서, 지원서, 간단한 대화 등과 같은 문서에 의해 안내될 것이다.

 ## See below for a sample one-on-one interview conversation: 샘플 1:1 면접 대화를 아래에서 참조하라.

Interviewer 1: Hello, Ms. Yuna Park. I am Jenny Walter, and my colleague is Peter Smith. We will be interviewing you this morning.

Interviewee: Hello, Ms. Walter and Mr. Smith. It is my pleasure to meet you.

Interviewer 2: Please sit down, Ms. Park.

Interviewee: Thank you, Mr. Smith. Please call me Yuna.

Interviewer 1: Yuna, could you briefly tell us something about yourself?

Interviewee: Sure. My name is Yuna Park and I recently graduated from _____ University this February, 2018. I have a degree in _____. Since my graduation, I have been working part-time at a family restaurant and taking an additional Chinese language course through a language academy. In the past, I also worked at a cafe for about a year. So I have about two years of work experience in the service industry. I have excellent teamwork and service skills as a result of my service experience.

Interviewer 1: Why are you taking a Chinese language course?

Interviewee: I am taking a Chinese language course to improve my language skills. I want to be able to speak three languages. I currently speak Korean and English.

Interviewer 2: How did you learn English? You speak English quite well.

Interviewee: Thank you for your compliment. I learned how to speak English through my language courses in college. I studied really hard to become a better speaker. I was also in a conversational English language club in college, which was very helpful.

Interviewer 2: How long have you been working at the family restaurant?

Interviewee: I have been working there since my third year in college. So I have been working there for about two years.

Interviewer 1: Have you had any difficulty while working there?

Interviewee: Well, in the beginning I sometimes faced unfriendly and demanding customers. At first, I didn't know how to treat them. However, as time passed by, I became more confident serving them and satisfying their needs.

Please also visit https://www.youtube.com/watch?v=96kT6WoATQE&t= 8s to view a sample one-on-one interview.

또한 https://www.youtube.com/watch?v=96kT6WoATQE&t=8s 를 방문하여 샘플 일 대일 인터뷰를 관찰하라.

Group Interview - A group interview is a screening process where multiple applicants are interviewed at the same time. Same questions may be often asked to the entire group or questions may be directed by each individual's application documents. This type of interview is very similar to the one-on-one interview above except that the interview is conducted with multiple interviewees.

그룹 면접 – 그룹 면접은 여러 명의 지원자가 동시에 인터뷰하는 심사 과정이다. 종종 동일한 질문이 그룹 전체에게 제시되거나 각 개인의 지원 서류로 질문이 제시될 수 있다. 이 유형의 인터뷰는 여러 명의 인터뷰 대상자와 진행된다는 점을 제외하고는 위의 일대일 인터뷰와 매우 유사하다.

Group Discussion - A group discussion may be sometimes referred to as a group activity. In this type of interview process, a topic or a situation is given to the group of candidates and the group is asked to discuss the topic among themselves. It is more important to demonstrate politeness and understanding during this activity than to boast your knowledge in the matter.

그룹 토론 – 그룹 토론은 그룹 활동 이라고도 한다. 이 유형의 면접 과정은 주제나 상황을 그룹 구성원들에게 제시하고 해당 주제에 대해 토론하도록 한다. 이러한 그룹 토론 에서 여러분의 지식을 자랑하는 것보다 예의와 이해심을 나타내는 것이 더 중요하다.

See the following group discussion tips.
다음 그룹 토론의 팁을 참조하라.

☑ Listen attentively to what others have to say.
다른 사람들의 말을 주의 깊게 경청하라.

☑ Even if you don't agree, demonstrate that you respect other people's perspectives.
동의하지 않더라도 다른 사람들의 관점을 존중한다는 것을 입증하라.

☑ Graciously accept differences of opinion.
다른 사람의 의견을 정중하게 수용하라.

☑ Be respectful and considerate when others speak.
다른 사람들이 말할 때 존중하고 배려하라.

☑ State your opinion clearly and logically when it is your time to state your perspective.
자신의 시각을 전달할 시간이 될 때 자신의 의견을 명확하고 논리적으로 기술하라.

☑ Be prepared to respond to follow-up questions or statements.
후속 질문이나 질문에 응답할 준비를 하라

☑ Do not dominate the discussion.
토론을 지배하지 마라.

☑ Be an active participant.
적극적인 참여자가 되라.

☑ Be polite and courteous.
공손하고 예의 바르게 토론에 참여 하라.

☑ Smile and maintain good eye contact when you speak and listen.
말하고 들을 때 눈을 잘 맞추고 미소지으며 유지하라.

☑ Acknowledge and affirm other opinions before you state yours.
당신의 의견을 전하기 전에 다른 의견을 인정하고 존중 하라.

☑ Have a sense of humor but do not make jokes.
유머 감각이 있지만 농담을 하지 마라.

☑ Do not use any offensive gestures.
불쾌감을 주는 제스처를 사용하지 마라.

☑ Be focused and stay on topic.
초점과 주제에 집중하라.

<u>**Article Summarization-**</u> Article summarization requires applicants to read a short article in English and to verbally summarize it.

<u>기사 요약</u> – 기사요약은 지원자들이 영어로 된 짧은 기사 글을 읽고 요약하도록 한다.

Article Summarization
기사 요약

Summaries are basically abridged versions of longer reading/writing pieces. They should include all the important main ideas stated in the original reading pieces without any additional information. Summaries are brief and minor details and examples are excluded. Good summaries tell the main ideas clearly from the original reading but in a condensed form.

요약은 기본적으로 장문의 읽기/쓰기 부분의 요약본이다. 추가 정보 없이 원본 독서 부분에 언급 된 중요한 모든 주요 아이디어를 포함해야한다. 요약은 간략하고 사소한 세부 사항이며 예제는 제외된다. 좋은 요약은 주요 아이디어를 원작과 명확하게 구분하지만 압축된 형태로 나타낸다.

Tips for Article Summarization
기사 요약을 위한 팁

Use the following tips when you summarize an article or a writing piece.

기사나 글쓰기를 요약 할 때 다음 팁을 사용하라.

- Read carefully the article you want to summarize (if necessary read it twice) 요약하려는 기사를 주의 깊게 읽다 (필요한 경우 두 번 읽음).
- Underline the main idea of the reading 독서의 주요 아이디어에 밑줄을 긋다
- Identify the supporting points for the main idea 주요 아이디어에 대한 지지 점을 확인한다.

- Using the key words or phrases, create sentences that state main ideas 핵심단어나 구절을 사용하여 주요 아이디어를 기술하는 문장을 만든다.
- Check to make sure that all main ideas are included 모든 주요 아이디어가 포함되어 있는지 확인하라
- Check to make sure that no additional information is added 추가 정보가 추가되지 않았는지 확인하라
- Use appropriate transitions to connect ideas 적절한 연결사를 사용하여 아이디어를 연결하라

 ## Here is a sample: 다음 샘플을 참조하라

Original Writing 원작

In general, job interviews can be stressful, and an airline job interview in English can be even more so as English is not the interviewee's native language. Prospective flight attendants not only have to prepare for a regular job interview process, but they also have to prepare for a job interview in foreign languages. The good news is that airline English interviews can be prepared. Studying the common airline interview questions and responses in English is one of the best ways to prepare for an English interview.

Sample Summary 샘플 요약

This reading states that English job interviews can be more stressful for those prospective interviewees where English is not their native language. But interviews in English can be prepared by studying the common job interview questions and responses in English.

Picture Description - Picture description requires applicants to view a photo and to describe it as is.

사진 설명 – 지원자가 제시되는 사진을 보고 그대로 묘사하도록 요구한다.

When you describe a picture, start with simple facts. First focus on the key items or people in the picture. Use the following questions and expressions when describing a photo.

그림을 묘사 할 때는 간단한 사실부터 시작하라. 먼저 주요 항목이나 그림의 사람들에게 초점을 맞춘다. 사진을 설명 할 때 다음 질문과 표현을 사용하라.

What do you see in the photo?

사진에 무엇이 보입니까?

In the photo I see _____
There is a _____ / There are _____

What is the person in the photo doing? What are the people in the photo doing? How is the weather?

사진 속 인물은 무엇입니까? 사진 속안에 있는 사람들은 무엇을 하고 있습니까?
날씨는 어때요?

The woman/man or girl/boy is ...ing.
The people are ...ing. The crowd is ...ing.
It's sunny. It's raining or snowing.

What do you see in the middle, in the front, or in the back of the picture?

사진 가운데, 앞 또는 뒤에는 무엇이 보이나요?

Next to...
In front of
Behind
On top of

What are the people in the photo wearing? Can you guess the weather or the season based on what they are wearing?

사진 속에 있는 사람들은 무엇을 입고 있습니까? 그들이 무엇을 입고 있는지에 따라 날씨
나 계절을 추측 할 수 있습니까?

<u>Say what people are wearing with the present continuous</u>

The woman/man or girl/boy is wearing.......

The people are wearing.......

The woman has a scarf around her neck.

The man is wearing a thick winter coat.

What can you guess from looking at people's actions?

사람들의 행동을 보면서 무엇을 추측 할 수 있습니까?

It looks like she is _____ .

It might be that he is _____ .

They could be ...ing _____ .

Perhaps everyone is _____ .

Does the picture remind you of anything? If so, what?

이 그림이 당신에게 어떤 것을 생각나게 합니까? 그렇다면, 무엇입니까?

The photo reminds me of when I _____.

This reminds me ...ing _____.

How does the picture make you feel?

이 그림이 당신을 어떻게 느끼게 합니까?

I feel happy looking at the photo because _____.

The picture makes me feel _____.

Here is a sample:

In this picture, I see a woman and a man with a dog. These two people are holding hands and walking the dog. In the back of the picture, I see a person riding a bicycle. It looks like they are on a walking trail. The weather seems sunny and nice. The woman and the man each have a thin jacket around her/his waist. Maybe they are a married couple. They look happy together. This photo reminds me of the time when I took a walk with my friend.

In-Flight Announcement- In-flight announcement reading tests require candidates to read in-flight announcements in English in addition to other relevant foreign languages.

기내방송 – 기내 방송 읽기 시험은 다른 관련 외국어 뿐만 아니라 영어로 기내 방송을 읽어야 한다.

Flight Announcement Tips
기내방송 팁

It is important to read flight announcements clearly and slowly. Pronounce and enunciate important pieces of information clearly and slowly. To develop a clear natural voice, practice vocal exercises. Practicing reading aloud and recording yourself when reading flight announcements are some of the simple ways to monitor your pronunciation, pace, and volume.

기내방송은 명확하고 차분하게 읽는 것이 중요하다. 중요한 정보를 명확하고 천천히 발음해야 한다. 밝고 경쾌하게 목소리를 개발하려면 연습을 해야 한다. 소리내어 읽기 및 녹음 연습을 하는 것은 방송을 읽을 때 발음, 속도 및 음량을 모니터링 하는 간단한 방법이다.

Sample Flight Announcements

1. Boarding Announcement 탑승 안내

Ladies and gentlemen,

Welcome aboard. This is _____ Air - flight _____ bound for Japan. Our flight time will be 1 hour and 20 minutes.

The captain has turned on the Fasten Seat Belt sign. Please make sure that your seat belt is fastened and your seat back and folding trays are in their full upright position. Please stow your carry-on luggage underneath the seat in front of you or in overhead bin. All electronic devices must be turned off during take-off and landing. We will be taking off shortly.

Please remember that this is a non-smoking flight. Smoking is strictly prohibited on the entire aircraft, including the lavatories. If you have any questions, please ask one of our flight attendants.

We hope you enjoy your flight with us. Thank you for flying _____ Air.

2. Safety Demonstration 안전 절차 시범

Ladies and gentlemen,

We will be showing our safety demonstration in a few minutes. Please direct your attention to the computer monitors in front of you. We would like your complete attention while the safety demonstration is showing.

We also strongly recommend you read all the safety information card located in the seat pocket in front of you before take-off. If you have any questions, please don't hesitate to ask one of our crew members. We wish you a pleasant flight.

3. Take-Off 이륙

Ladies and gentlemen,

We are first in priority for take-off, we should depart in a couple of minutes. Please make sure your seat belt is securely fastened.

Cabin crew, please take your seats for take-off.

4. Turbulence 기류 변화

Ladies and gentlemen,

We are passing through an area of turbulence. The captain has turned on the seat belt sign on. Please fasten your seat belt and keep it fastened until the captain turns off the seat belt sign.

5. Landing 착륙

Ladies and gentlemen,

Welcome to _____ International airport. Local time here in _____ is 9:30 A.M. in the morning on Wednesday the 3rd of March. The temperature is 60 degrees in fahrenheit.

For your safety and comfort, please remain seated with your seat belt fastened until the captain turns off the seat belt sign. Once the Fasten Seat Belt sign has been turned off, cellular phones may be used.

Please use caution when opening the overhead bins as contents may have moved during the flight. Also please check around your seat and in your seat pocket to make sure no personal belongings are left behind you.

On behalf of the entire crew, we would like to thank you for flying _____ Air. We look forward to seeing you again in the near future. Have a pleasant day!

Please visit the following webpage to read, to practice, and to listen to sample flight announcements.

다음 웹 페이지를 방문하여 기내방속 예시를 읽고, 연습하고, 들어라.

https://www.englishclub.com/english-for-work/airline-announcements.htm

 Let's Practice English · 영어를 연습해 보자

Activity 1: Reading/Writing/Speaking 읽기/쓰기/말하기

Provide a variety of photos to students. Have students view the photos and describe them. Do this activity as a group activity. Have each group share what they wrote.

학생들에게 다양한 사진을 제공하라. 학생들에게 사진을 보고 설명하게 하라. 이 활동을 그룹 활동으로 만들어라. 각 그룹에게 그들이 쓴 것을 이야기 하게 하라.

Activity 2: Listening/Speaking 듣기/말하기

Do a mock group interview. Select students to be interviewers and interviewees. Use the warm-up questions to do the practice interview.

샘플 그룹 모의 인터뷰를 하라. 면접관과 면접자가 될 학생을 선택하라. 워밍업 질문을 사용하여 연습 인터뷰를 하라.

Q.1 Is your name _____? Can I have your name and number, please?

당신의 이름은 _____입니까?

당신의 이름과 응시 번호를 알려줄 수 있을까요?

Q.2 How are you today? How are you feeling today?

오늘 기분이 어떠세요?

Q.3 Where are you from?

어느 나라 사람인가요?

Q.4 Did you have any difficulty finding this place?

이 장소를 찾는데 어려움이 있었습니까?

Q.5 Where do you currently live?

지금 사는 곳이 어디입니까?

Q.6 How do you maintain good health?

건강관리를 어떻게 하시나요?

Q.7 What is your current job?

현재 무슨 일을 하나요?

Q.8 Have you applied for _____ Airline before?

전에 _____ 항공을 신청하셨습니까?

Q.9 What do you know about our airline?

우리 항공사에 대해 무엇을 아십니까?

Q.10 Is your phone number _____? Could we call you later today for the next assessment process?

전화번호는 _____입니까?

다음 평가 절차를 위해 오늘 늦게 전화 할 수 있습니까?

Success in English Interview for Cabin Crew: How to Win the Job Interview

항공 승무원을 위한 성공 영어 인터뷰:
면접에서 승리하는 방법

Chapter 03

Improving Your Self-Introduction
자기소개 개선하기

Chapter 03

Improving Your Self-Introduction
자기소개 개선하기

 Chapter Goals 챕터 목표

✹ To use appropriate expressions to confidently introduce yourself
적절한 표현을 사용하여 자신을 자신있게 소개하기

✹ To appropriately use the correct tense: simple past or present perfect
올바른 시제를 적절하게 사용하기: 단순 과거 또는 현재 완료

 Grammar Points 핵심 문법

Use the simple past tense to describe an action or state that was completed in the past, especially when the specific time is mentioned.

특히 특정 시간이 언급되었을 때 단순 과거 시제를 사용하여 과거에 완료된 행동이나 상태를 설명한다.

Use the present perfect tense (have/has + past participle) to talk about an action that happened sometime in the past but is still relevant in the present. We often use 'for' or 'since' with the present perfect tense.

불특정한 과거에 시작되어 현재까지 계속되는 일에 대해 이야기하기 위해 현재 완료 시제 (have / has + past 분사)를 사용한다. 우리는 종종 현재 완료 시제와 'for' 또는 'since'를 사용한다.

Key Vocabulary 주요 어휘

maintain	improve	beneficial
similarities	aware of	socialize
practical	acquired	task
pertinent	inform	varied
develop	effective	coworkers

Key Expressions 핵심 표현

See each section for key expressions.

각 부분에서 핵심 표현을 참조하라.

🖥 Interview Tips 면접 팁 •

Asking job candidates to talk about themselves is perhaps the most common interview question in a job interview. When interviewers ask, "Tell me about yourself," this is not the time to talk about your hobbies or personal stories. Your response should be focused and pertinent to the job you are interviewing for. Talking about yourself is the perfect opportunity for you to highlight your strengths. Focus on your pertinent experiences, skills, and/or personality traits to demonstrate that you are the right person for the job.

취업 응시자에게 자신에 대해 이야기 하기를 요구하는 것은 아마도 취업 면접에서 가장 일반적인 면접 질문일 것이다. 면접관이 "당신에 대해 말해보세요"라고 물으면, 이것은 취미나 개인적인 이야기에 대해 말하는 시간이 아니다. 당신의 답변은 당신이 인터뷰하는 직업에 중점을 두어야 한다. 자신에 대해 말하는 것은 자신의 강점을 강조할 수 있는 완벽한 기회이다. 자신의 적절한 경험, 기술 및 / 또는 성격에 초점을 맞추어 자신이 직업에 적합한 사람임을 입증하라.

> **Use the following tips to create your own successful self-introduction:**
> 다음 팁을 사용하여 자신만의 성공적인 자기 소개를 만들어라

Start with a simple "thank you." Before beginning your self-introduction, thank the interviewers for the opportunity to interview with them. Companies do not interview every applicant, so be grateful for the interview opportunity. This also illustrates how enthusiastic you are about the job opportunity with them.

간단하게 "감사합니다"로 시작하라. 자기소개를 시작하기 전에 면접관에게 인터뷰 기회를 주셔서 감사하다는 말을 전하라. 회사는 모든 지원자와 면접하지 않으므로 면접 기회에 감사를 표시하는 것이다. 이것은 또한 당신이 가진 취업 기회에 관하여 얼마나 열정적인지 보여준다.

Be focused and be selective with the information you provide. Do not provide complete personal or employment history. Select the experience that is most pertinent and important for the job. Your response should inform the interviewer that you are the right person for the job.

집중하고 제공하는 정보를 스스로 선택하라. 완전한 개인정보 또는 경력을 제공하지 말라. 이 직업에 가장 적절하고 중요한 경험을 선택한다. 당신의 답변은 면접관에게 당신이 그 일에 적합한 사람이라는 것을 알려 주어야한다.

Make yourself a desirable and suitable candidate. Focus on your education, professional work/volunteer experiences, and skills relevant to the job you are applying.

자신을 바람직하고 적합한 지원자로 만들어라. 당신의 교육, 전문직업 / 자원봉사자 경험, 그리고 당신이 지원한 직무와 관련된 기술에 초점을 맞추어야 한다.

> **Include the following information** • 다음 정보를 포함하라

1) Educational Details
   교육 내용
2) Current & Previous Job Experiences (Select the pertinent job experiences)
   현재와 이전 직업경험 (관련 직업 경험을 선택하라)
3) Skills Gained or Accomplishments Achieved (From job or volunteer experience)
   획득한 기술 또는 달성한 성취 (직업 또는 자원 봉사 경험을 통해)
4) Positive personality traits (Select the most relevant and useful for the job you
   are applying)
   긍정적인 성격 특성 (지원하는 직업에 가장 관련이 있고 유용한 성격을 선택하라).

Practice, practice, and practice. Your self-introduction should sound
natural and polished.

연습, 연습 그리고 연습을 해라. 본인의 자기소개는 자연스럽고 우아하게 들려야 한다.

Sample Responses for Educational Details
교육 내용에 대한 응답 샘플

R1 I am currently attending _____ and majoring in _____.
저는 현재 _____에 다니고 있으며 _____를 전공하고 있습니다.

R2 I recently graduated from _____. I studied _____.
저는 최근에 _____에서 졸업했습니다. 저는 _____을 공부했습니다.

R3 I went to _____ and completed a degree in _____.
저는 _____에 갔고 _____에서 학위를 마쳤습니다.

R4 I am a recent graduate from _____. I studied _____.
저는 최근 _____ 졸업생입니다. 저는 _____를 공부했습니다.

Sample Responses for Study Abroad Experiences
해외 학업 경험(어학연수, 교환학생)에 대한 응답 샘플

R1 I studied in New Zealand as an exchange student for one year. I learned so much from that experience. I feel very comfortable and confident to speak English and to approach foreigners.

저는 교환 학생으로 뉴질랜드에서 1년간 공부했습니다. 그 경험에서 많은 것을 배웠습니다. 저는 영어로 말하고 외국인에게 접근하는 것이 매우 편안하고 자신감을 느낍니다.

R2 Our school offered different study abroad programs, so I had an opportunity to study in China for one semester. I gained so much from that experience as my Chinese improved tremendously. Also, because of my study abroad experience, I am more appreciative of different cultures.

우리 학교는 해외 유학 프로그램을 다양하게 제공했으므로 한 학기 동안 중국에서 공부 할 수 있는 기회가 있었습니다. 나는 그 경험에서 많은 것을 얻었고 또한 중국어도 대단히 향상 되었습니다. 또한 해외 유학 경험 때문에 다른 문화에 대해 더 감사하게 생각합니다.

R3 My study abroad and travel experiences in various countries have helped me learn their languages and cultures. I studied in Japan for one year and was able to travel to various English speaking countries such as Canada, the United States, and New Zealand. I can speak both English and Japanese quite well.

다양한 나라에서의 나의 유학 경험과 여행 경험은 내가 그들의 언어와 문화를 배우는데 도움이 되었습니다. 일본에서 1 년간 공부했으며 캐나다, 미국, 뉴질랜드 등 다양한 영어권 국가를 여행 할 수 있었습니다. 나는 영어와 일본어를 모두 잘 할 수 있습니다.

Sample Responses for Current & Previous Job Experiences
현재 & 이전 직무 경험에 대한 응답 샘플

R1 I previously worked at a hotel and obtained useful experience from it. I learned a great deal of working with various customers and providing high-quality service.

이전에 호텔에서 일했고 유용한 경험을 얻었습니다. 저는 다양한 고객과의 협력과 양질의 서비스 제공에 대해 많은 것을 배웠습니다.

R2 I have various work experiences in the service industry. For example, I worked in different places such as a restaurant, a hotel, and a clothing store. Having these experiences allowed me to enhance communication and interpersonal skills.

저는 서비스 업계에서 다양한 업무 경험을 쌓았습니다. 예를 들어 레스토랑, 호텔, 옷 가게 등 다양한 장소에서 일했습니다. 이러한 경험을 통해 소통 및 대인관계 기술을 향상시킬 수 있었습니다.

R3 I have more than two years of work experience in the service field. As a result, I am very confident in working with various customers and meeting their needs.

저는 서비스 분야에서 2년 이상의 경력을 쌓았습니다. 결과적으로, 다양한 고객과 협력하고 그들의 요구를 충족시키는데 매우 자신감이 생겼습니다.

Sample Responses for Skills Gained or Accomplishments Achieved 획득 한 기술 또는 달성 한 성과에 대한 응답 샘플

R1 Working at a department store for more than two years enabled me to serve a wide variety of customers. As a result, I gained effective communication and interpersonal skills.

백화점에서 2년 이상 일하면서 다양한 고객에게 서비스를 제공 할 수 있었습니다. 그 결과, 나는 효과적인 의사소통과 대인관계 기술을 습득하게 되었습니다.

R2 My work experiences in the various service industries have helped me become professional and polite. I am respectful, understanding, and sensitive to all customers and situations.

다양한 서비스 업계에서 근무한 경험으로 저는 전문성과 공손함을 배웠습니다. 저는 모든 고객을 존중하고 이해하며 상황에 민감합니다.

R3 As a result of my work experience in a hotel, I have gained excellent teamwork skills. I am very cooperative and work well with others.

호텔에서 근무한 경험으로 탁월한 팀워크 기술을 습득했습니다. 저는 매우 협조적이며 다른 사람들과 잘 어울립니다.

Sample Responses for Positive Personality Traits 긍정적인 성격에 대한 응답 샘플

R1 I am an excellent problem solver. I have an ability to detect problems and find appropriate solutions. I feel I have this ability because I am very attentive and decisive.

저는 훌륭한 문제해결자입니다. 문제를 감지하고 적절한 해결책을 찾을 수 있는 능력이 있습니다. 매우 세심하고 결정적이기 때문에 저는 이 능력을 가지고 있다고 느낍니다.

R2 I am a responsible and hard working individual. When it comes to completing any task for work or for school, I have always been dedicated and committed to producing high-quality work.

저는 책임있고 열심히 일하는 사람입니다. 직장이나 학교에 대한 모든 작업에 관해서, 저는 항상 전념하고 고품질의 성과를 창출하기 위해 최선을 다하고 있습니다.

R3 I have been told that I am a people person. I work well with others and I always try to help my co-workers whenever they need help.

저는 제가 사교적인 사람이라는 말을 들었습니다. 저는 다른 사람들과 잘 지내며 항상 도움이 필요할 때마다 동료들을 도우려고 노력합니다.

Sample Responses for Concluding Statements
결론 문장에 대한 응답 샘플

R1 I would like to use my service skills to serve both your airline and your passengers.

귀하의 항공사와 승객 모두를 위해 저의 서비스 기술을 사용하고 싶습니다.

R2 It would be an honor if I am part of your company. I look forward to utilizing my abilities to dedicate myself.

제가 귀사에 속하게 된다면 영광입니다. 저는 제 자신을 헌신하고 제 능력을 활용하기를 기대합니다.

R3 I believe my strengths and work experience will be useful when I work as a flight attendant. Thank you for your time and this opportunity.

제가 승무원으로 일하게 된다면 저의 강점과 근무 경험이 유용할 것으로 믿습니다. 귀한 시간과 이 기회에 감사드립니다.

R4 I believe I have the positive traits that are suitable for this position.

저는 이 직책에 적합한 긍정적인 특성을 가지고 있다고 믿습니다.

R5 I am very passionate about this job opportunity. I hope to make valuable contributions to your airline.

저는 이 직책에 대해 열정적입니다. 저는 귀하의 항공사에 소중한 기여를 하기를 희망합니다.

R6 If I become a member of your airline, I will give my 100% to provide the best performance.

만약 제가 귀하의 항공사의 직원이 되면 최고 성과를 수행하기 위해 100% 최선을 다할 것 입니다.

R7 Thank you very much for your time.

시간 내주셔서 대단히 감사합니다.

R8 I sincerely appreciate your time.

진심으로 감사드립니다.

Interview Questions
면접 질문

Q.1 Would you please tell me about yourself?

당신에 대해서 말해 주시겠습니까?

Q.2 Tell me about yourself.

당신에 대해 말해주세요.

Q.3 Can you introduce yourself?

당신 소개 좀 해줄래요?

Q.4 Could you tell us about yourself?

당신에 대해서 말해 주시겠습니까?

Q.5 What don't you tell us about yourself?

당신에 대해 우리에게 말해 주시겠습니까?

🖼️ Interview Tips 면접 팁 •

Review the job description and identify the essential skills that the employer is looking for in a prospective job candidate. Incorporate that information when you think of your introduction. This will help you become a more viable candidate for the position.

직무 기술서로 검토하고 고용주가 입사 지원자에게서 찾고자 하는 필수적인 기술을 확인하시오. 자기소개를 할 때 그 정보를 포함시킨다. 이것은 당신이 그 직책에 대해 더 유력한 후보가 될 수 있도록 도와 줄 것이다.

🗣️ Interview Questions & Sample Responses
면접 질문 및 응답 샘플

Q.1 Would you please tell me about yourself?

당신에 대해서 말해 주시겠습니까?

I am very grateful to introduce myself. My name is _____. I am currently attending _____ and majoring in airline service. This is my last semester and I will be graduating in February 2019. I would like to describe myself as a responsible and dedicated person. While attending college, I have also held a sales position at a cosmetics store working every weekend for the last two years. In addition, I have been involved in my school extracurricular activity and held a leadership position. Even though I was quite busy at school and at work, I have never missed school or work. I have also maintained excellent grades. I believe these qualities will be useful when I become a member of your company. I will be a dedicated and committed cabin crew who always thinks of the company and its passengers first.

이렇게 저를 소개할 수 있어서 참 기쁩니다. 저의 이름은 _____ 입니다. 저는 현재 _____에 다니며 항공 서비스를 전공하고 있습니다. 지금 마지막 학기이고 저는 2019년 2월 졸업할 예정입니다. 저는 책임있고 헌신적인 사람으로 제 자신을 묘사하고 싶습니다. 대학에 다닐 때, 지난 2년 동안 주말마다 화장품 가게에서 판매사원으로 근무했습니다. 또한, 저는 학교 활동에 참여하여 지도력을 발휘했습니다. 학교와 직장에서 바빴지만 학교나 직장을 한번도 결석한 적이 없습니다. 저는 또한 우수한 성적을 유지했습니다. 이 자질들이 제가 귀하의 회사직원이 될 때 유용 할 것이라고 믿습니다. 저는 회사와 승객을 항상 생각하는 헌신적인 승무원이 될 것입니다.

Q.2 Tell me about yourself.
당신에 대해 말해주세요.

Good morning. I am very happy to meet you. My name is _____ but you can call me Cathy. Ever since I was young, I have always been interested in other languages and cultures. So I majored in English and Chinese from _____ University. I have also had opportunities to study both in Canada and in China through study abroad programs. Because of these study abroad experiences, my language skills in English and Chinese improved tremendously. But I have also become more appreciative of other cultures, and I am aware of differences and similarities among them. My greatest strength is having a good sense of flexibility and adaptability. I truly enjoy experiencing and learning about different people and cultures. I can also easily socialize and make friends with all different types of people. I would like to use my skills to make a positive contribution to your company.

좋은 아침입니다. 만나서 반갑습니다. 제 이름은 ＿＿＿＿＿＿＿ 이지만 캐시라고 불러도 됩니다. 저는 어렸을 때부터 항상 다른 언어와 문화에 관심이 있었습니다. 그래서 저는 ＿＿＿＿＿＿＿ 대학에서 영어와 중국어를 전공했습니다. 저는 유학 프로그램을 통해 캐나다와 중국에서 공부할 수 있는 기회도 얻었습니다. 이러한 유학 경험을 통해 영어와 중국어의 언어 실력이 크게 향상되었습니다. 그러나 저는 또한 다른 문화를 더 감사하게 생각하고 그 차이점과 유사점을 알고 있습니다. 저의 가장 큰 강점은 융통성과 적응력의 좋은 감각을 가지고 있는 것입니다. 저는 진정으로 다양한 사람들과 문화에 대한 경험과 학습을 즐깁니다. 저는 또한 쉽게 사교적으로 서로 다른 유형의 사람들과 친구가 될 수 있습니다. 귀하의 회사에 긍정적인 기여를 하기 위해 제 능력을 사용하고 싶습니다.

Q.3 Can you introduce yourself?
당신 소개 좀 해줄래요?

Thank you for this opportunity to introduce myself. I studied tourism management from ＿＿＿＿＿＿＿ University. My major was very helpful and practical, and I learned a lot from it. Through my major, I have gained useful knowledge and service skills in the service industry. While in college, I also had various part-time jobs, such as working at a wedding hall, a restaurant, and a cafe. I am still working at the cafe. Because of these working experiences, I have acquired important interpersonal and teamwork skills. I have been told by my previous supervisors that I work well with co-workers and customers. Because of this trait, I was also given the opportunity to train new employees at my previous work place. I would like to use my skills to serve both your airline and your passengers.

저에게 소개 할 수 있는 기회를 주셔서 감사합니다. 저는 ＿＿＿＿＿＿＿ 대학에서 관광 경영학을 전공했습니다. 전공은 매우 유익하고 실용적이었고 많은 것을 배웠습니다. 전공을 통해 서비스 업계에서 유용한 지식과 서비스 기술을 습득했습니다. 대학에 다니는 동안 저는 또한 결혼식장, 식당 및 카페에서 일하는 것과 같은 다양한 아르바이트를 경험 했습니다. 저는 아직도 카페에서 일하고 있습니다. 이러한 경험 덕분에 저는 중요한 대인관계 및 팀워크 기술을 습득했습니다. 이전 동료 그리고 상사들로 부터 동료나 고객들과 잘 어울린다는 말을 들었습니다. 이러한 특성으로 인해 이전 직장에서 신입 사원을 교육 할 기회를 얻었습니다. 귀하의 항공사와 승객 모두를 위해 저의 기술을 사용하고 싶습니다.

Q.4 Could you tell us about yourself?
당신에 대해서 말해 주시겠습니까?

Hello. It's great to meet you. My name is _____. I have a _____ degree from _____ University. I would like to describe myself as a disciplined and committed person. I take great pride in my work, so when I am given projects or tasks through my work or through my school, I always give my best performance. I believe being disciplined has helped me succeed at school and at work. In the past, I have received academic scholarships from my college and positive feedback from my previous supervisors. If I become a member of your airline, I will always give my 100% to provide the best quality work. Thank you.

안녕하세요. 만나 뵙게 되어 기쁩니다. 제 이름은 _____ 라고 합니다. 저는 _____ 대학에서 _____ 학위를 받았습니다. 저는 제 자신을 훈련되고 헌신적인 사람으로 묘사하고 싶습니다. 저는 제 일에 큰 자부심을 가지고 있습니다. 그래서 일이나 학교를 통해 프로젝트 일을 할 때 항상 최선을 다합니다. 저는 훈련된 제 모습이 학교와 직장에서 성공하는 데 도움이 되었다고 생각합니다. 과거에는 대학에서 학업 장학금을 받았고 이전 상사로부터 긍정적인 피드백을 받았습니다. 제가 귀사의 직원이 된다면 최고의 품질을 제공하기 위해 항상 100% 최선을 다할 것입니다. 고맙습니다.

Q.5 Why don't you tell us something about yourself?

당신에 대해 우리에게 말해 주시겠습니까?

My name is _____. I recently graduated from _____ University and studied _____. My major was useful and beneficial for me as I acquired foreign language skills, effective communication skills, and practical service knowledge. While in college, I also worked several part-time jobs in the service industry. For example, I worked at Baskin-Robbins and several fast food restaurants. Having these varied experiences have helped me to feel confident about myself and to develop an ability to work with all kinds of customers. I believe that I would make an important contribution to your company. Thank you.

제 이름은 _____라고 합니다. 저는 최근에 _____ 대학을 졸업하고 _____을 공부했습니다. 저의 전공은 외국어 기술, 효과적인 의사소통 기술 및 실천적인 서비스 지식을 습득했기 때문에 유용하고 유익했습니다. 대학에 다니는 동안 저는 또한 서비스 산업에서 여러가지 파트타임 일을 했습니다. 예를 들어 Baskin-Robbins 와 여러 패스트푸드 레스토랑에서 일했습니다. 이러한 다양한 경험을 통해 제 자신에 대해 자신감을 갖고 모든 다양한 고객과 일할 수 있는 능력을 키울 수 있었습니다. 저는 귀하의 회사에 중요한 기여를 할 것이라고 믿습니다. 감사합니다.

Your Response: 당신의 대답

Let's Practice English · 영어를 연습해 보자

Activity 1: Writing/Speaking/Listening 쓰기/말하기/듣기

Use the following topics to find more information about your partner. Create relevant questions to the topics and ask those questions to your partner.

아래의 주제를 사용하여 파트너에 대한 자세한 정보를 찾아라. 주제를 사용하여 관련된 질문을 만들고 파트너에게 질문하라.

Topic 1: Educational Details 교육 내용
Topic 2: Current & Previous Job Experiences 현재와 이전 직업경험
Topic 3: Skills Gained or Accomplishments Achieved 기술습득 또는 달성한 성취
Topic 4: Positive Personality Traits 긍정적인 성격 특성

Example with topic 1: Educational Details

You: What is your major? Where do you go to school? What courses are you taking?

Partner: My major is _____. I go to _____ University. I am taking _____ and _____ courses.

Example with topic 2: Job Experiences

You: Do you currently work?
Partner: Yes, I work at a cafe.
You: What do you do there?
Partner: I sell beverages and dessert to customers.

Activity 2: Writing/Speaking 쓰기/말하기

Please answer the following questions. Share your responses with your partner.
다음 질문에 답하라. 파트너에게 답변을 공유하라.

1. Have you been abroad to study English or any foreign language? If so, tell me about the experience.

2. Do you have any job experience? Please tell me about your job experience.

3. What skills have you gained from your work experience?

4. What is your greatest strength?

Success in English Interview for Cabin Crew:
How to Win the Job Interview

항공 승무원을 위한 성공 영어 인터뷰:
면접에서 승리하는 방법

Chapter 04

General English Interview Questions
일반적인 영어 면접 질문

Chapter 04

General English Interview Questions
일반적인 영어 면접 질문

Chapter Goals 챕터 목표

⚹ To identify common English interview questions
일반적인 영어 면접 질문 확인하기

⚹ To use appropriate expressions to respond to common English interview questions
적절한 표현들을 사용하여 일반적인 영어 면접 질문에 대답하기

⚹ To differentiate and identify main verbs and helping verbs in questions
질문에서 주동사와 조동사를 구별하고 확인하기

Grammar Points 핵심 문법

The Present Tense 현재시제

Use the simple present tense verbs when talking about actions in the present that do not usually change. See the following different uses of the present tense:

지속적으로 반복되는 현재의 상태나 동작에 대해 이야기 할 때 동사의 단순 현재 시제를 사용하라. 다음과 같이 다양하게 쓰이는 현재 시제를 참조하라.

Present Habits: I often exercise on weekends. My niece always takes a nap in the afternoon. I usually do not eat breakfast.

현재의 습관 : 저는 주말에 운동을 자주합니다. 저의 조카는 항상 오후에 낮잠을 자요.
　　　　　나는 보통 아침 식사를 하지 않습니다.

Opinions and Feelings: I enjoy eating spicy food. My boss does not like drinking coffee.

의견 및 느낌: 나는 매운 음식 먹는 것을 즐깁니다.
　　　　　사장님은 커피 마시는 것을 좋아하지 않습니다.

General Facts and Truths: Many graduates worry about finding a job after they graduate.

일반적인 사실과 진리: 많은 졸업생들은 졸업 후에 직업을 찾는 것에 대하여 걱정합니다.

Helping Verbs 조동사

Helping verbs or sometimes called auxiliary verbs are verbs that help the main verb in a sentence by expanding the meaning of the verb. They can add specific detail how time is shown in a sentence. There are 13 verbs that are used as helping verbs in English.

조동사는 동사의 의미를 확장하여 문장에서 본동사를 돕는 역할을 하는 동사로써 문장에 시간이 표시되는 방식에 따라 특정 세부 사항을 추가 할 수 있다. 다음과 같은 13 개의 조동사가 사용된다.

1. be (including am, is, are, was, were, been)
2. have, has, had
3. do, does, did
4. can
5. could
6. may
7. might

8. will

9. would

10. shall

11. should

12. must

13. ought to

These different helping verbs cannot form sentences or questions without main verbs. These helping verbs are used for different purposes in sentences. But one of the main purposes is to demonstrate the action of a sentence in a particular aspect of time. For example, in the following sentence, 'I am currently working at a local bank', indicates that the speaker is currently working at the local bank. The second function is to add the meaning of the main verb. In this sentence, 'I can work tomorrow', shows that the speaker is able to work tomorrow.

조동사는 주동사 없이 문장이나 질문을 만들 수 없다. 조동사는 문장에서 다른 용도로 사용된다. 그러나 주요 목적 중 하나는 특정한 시간의 측면에서 문장의 행동을 설명하는 것이다. 예를 들어, '나는 현재 지방 은행에서 일하고 있습니다.'라고 말하는 사람이 현재 지역 은행에서 일하고 있다는 것을 나타낸다. 두 번째 기능은 본동사의 의미를 추가하는 것이다. '내일 일할 수 있어요.'라고 말하는 사람이 내일 일할 수 있다는 것을 보여 준다.

Key Vocabulary 주요 어휘

command	overcame	appreciate
enormous	conflict	maintain
sophisticated	consecutively	align
diversity	advancement	path
accomplish	reputable	assets
deadlines	consider	practical

Key Expressions 핵심 표현

See each section for key expressions.

각 부분에서 핵심 표현을 참조하라.

Interview Tips 면접 팁 ·

It is always good to have your answers ready for the most common English interview questions. You should also practice them without making them sound rehearsed. You want your responses to come out as naturally and smoothly as possible.

가장 일반적인 영어 인터뷰 질문에 대한 답변을 준비하는 것이 좋다. 질문에 대한 답변이 자연스럽고 부드럽게 들릴 수 있도록 연습해야한다.

Interview Questions 면접 질문

Q.1 Tell me briefly about yourself.
자신에 대하여 간단하게 말해 보세요.

Q.2 Why should we hire you?
왜 우리가 당신을 고용해야 하나요?

Q.3 Why do you want to work here?
당신은 왜 우리 회사에서 일하기를 원합니까?

Q.4 Where do you see yourself in five years?
당신은 5년 후 어떤 모습으로 있기를 원합니까?

Q.5 Do you have any questions for us?
우리에게 질문이 있습니까?

Interview Questions & Sample Responses
면접 질문 및 응답 샘플

Q.1 Tell me briefly about yourself.
당신에 대하여 간단하게 말해 보세요..

R1 I would like to first thank you for this opportunity to interview with you. My name is _____. I have a degree in _____ from _____ University. After I graduated from college, I went abroad to further study English. While taking college-level English language courses in overseas, I also worked part-time at a family restaurant. At first, I had challenges living and working abroad. I did not have the best command of English, and I did not have a full understanding of cultural differences. However, I overcame these difficulties by working hard to improve English and to appreciate cultural differences. Living abroad for over a year has provided valuable experience for me to easily adapt in new places and to welcome any situations. My experiences have helped me become a positive and flexible person. I believe that my education and overseas experience will be useful when I work for your company.

먼저 귀사에서 인터뷰 기회를 주신 것에 대하여 감사하다고 말씀 드리고 싶습니다. 저의 이름은 _____ 이라고 합니다. 저는 _____ 대학에서 학위를 받았습니다. 대학을 졸업 한 후에, 저는 영어를 더 공부하기 위해 해외로 갔습니다. 해외에서 대학 수준의 영어 강의를 듣는 동안, 저는 패밀리 레스토랑에서 시간제로 근무도 하였습니다. 처음에는 해외에서 일하고 생활하는데 어려움을 겪었습니다. 저는 영어를 뛰어나게 잘하지도 못했고, 문화적 차이를 제대로 이해하지도 못했었습니다. 하지만 영어 실력을 향상시키고 문화적 차이를 이해하기 위하여 열심히 노력함으로

써 이러한 어려움들을 극복 하였습니다. 1년 넘게 해외에서 살다 보니 새로운 곳에 어렵지 않게 적응하고 어떤 상황이든 받아들일 수 있는 소중한 경험이 되었습니다. 이러한 경험은 제가 긍정적이고 유연한 사람이 될 수 있는 도움이 되었습니다. 제가 귀사에서 근무할 때 저의 교육과 해외 경험이 도움이 될 것으로 믿습니다.

R2 Thank you for this opportunity to introduce myself. It is truly an honor for me to be here. I am _____ from Seoul, Korea. I would like to describe myself as an energetic and active person, who has always welcomed new situations. While going to college, I was involved in a lot of school activities, and I excelled in them. For example, I became a key member of my school public representative committee and took different responsibilities of organizing school events. Some of these events required enormous amount of time, which conflicted with exam schedules. However, I never missed deadlines or important duties for any of the school events or academic work. I maintained excellent grades and worked as an active team member in the school events. I hope to apply these same qualities when I work for your company. Thank you again.

제 소개를 할 수 있는 기회를 주셔서 감사드립니다. 여기에 오게 되어 정말 영광입니다. 저는 서울에서 온 _____입니다. 저는 저를 활동적이고 적극적인 사람으로 설명하고 싶습니다. 대학에 다니는 동안, 저는 많은 학교 활동에 참여하였고, 그 활동에서 뛰어난 역량을 발휘 하였습니다. 예를 들어, 저는 우리 학교의 홍보부에서 중요한 대표가 되었고, 학교 행사를 준비하는 다양한 책임을 맡았습니다. 이러한 행사들 중 일부는 상당히 많은 시간이 필요 했으며 이는 시험 일정과 겹치기도 하였습니다. 하지만, 저는 학교의 행사나 학업에 있어서 마감일이나 중요한 임무를 결코 어느 것도 놓친 적이 없었습니다. 학교 행사에도 적극적인 팀원으로 일하면서도 좋은 성적을 유지하였습니다. 제가 귀사에서 일할 때도 이와 같은 자질을 적용하고 싶습니다. 다시 한 번 감사드립니다.

R3 Good afternoon, sir or madam. First, I would like to thank you for your time. I am very honored to be here. I have recently graduated from _____ University with a _____ degree. I also have over three years of service experience working at a wedding hall. In this capacity, I gained excellent service and communication skills dealing with a variety of customers in different situations. With a degree in _____ and service working experience, I have both theoretical and practical knowledge in the service industry, which will be valuable for your company. I hope to make positive contributions to your company.

안녕하십니까, 면접관님. 우선 시간을 내어 주신것에 감사드립니다. 저는 지금 이곳에 있게 되어 매우 영광입니다. 저는 최근에 _____ 대학을 졸업 하였습니다. 또한 저는 결혼식장에서 3년 이상 근무한 경험이 있습니다. 이러한 능력으로 다양한 상황에서 다양한 고객을 상대하는 뛰어난 서비스와 커뮤니케이션 기술을 습득 하였습니다. _____ 대학의 학위와 서비스 실무 경험을 가진 저는 귀사의 유용한 서비스 업계에 대한 이론적 지식과 실용적 지식을 모두 가지고 있습니다. 귀사에 긍정적인 공헌을 하기를 소망합니다.

Your Response: 당신의 대답

Q.2 Why should we hire you?

왜 우리가 당신을 고용해야 하나요?

🖥 Interview Tips 면접 팁 •

When thinking of answers to the "why should we hire you?" question, first review what is required in the job description or in the position in which you are applying. Come up with the response that includes what the company is desiring. For example, if the company is looking for someone who has specific personality traits or skills, you should include the qualities you have that suit the company's requirements. For each quality you have, think of a specific experience that could support that trait. If you also have a special certification that could make you stand out, it is helpful to include that information.

"왜 우리가 당신을 고용해야 하는가?"라는 질문에 대한 답을 생각할 때, 먼저 업무 설명이나 당신이 지원하는 위치에 무엇이 필요한지를 검토하라. 그리고 그 회사가 추구하고 원하는 바가 반영되어 있는 대답을 해라. 예를 들어, 회사에서 특별한 개성이나 기술을 가진 사람을 찾고 있다면 회사의 요구 사항에 맞는 특징을 대답에 포함 시켜야 한다. 자신이 가지고 있는 각각의 자질에 대한 특성을 뒷받침 할 수 있는 구체적인 경험에 대해서 생각해 보아라. 만약 당신이 눈에 띄는 특별한 인증을 받았을 경우, 그 정보를 포함하는 것이 도움이 된다.

R1 I believe I am the right person you need for your company. I have both educational and service experiences related to the job of cabin crew. I graduated with an airline service major and took many relevant courses that would be useful to work in the airline industry. I also have more than two years of job experience working at a department store. In that environment, I worked with a variety of customers which helped me gained excellent service skills. I will be a dedicated and attentive flight attendant.

저는 귀하의 회사에 필요한 사람이라고 생각합니다. 저는 항공 승무원의 직업과 관련된 교육 및 서비스 경험이 있습니다. 저는 항공서비스 전공으로 졸업을 하였고 항공 업계에서 일하는 데 유용한 많은 관련 강좌를 수강 하였습니다. 또한 백화점에서 2 년 이상의 경력을 쌓았습니다. 그 환경에서 저는 다양한 고객들을 위해 일을 했고 훌륭한 고객 서비스 기술을 습득하게 되었습니다. 저는 세심하고 친절한 항공 승무원이 될 것입니다.

R2 I have obtained sophisticated service skills that align with your company values from my previous job experience. I believe my skill set seems to be a perfect match for what you are looking for in this position. In addition, I work well with people and have excellent teamwork skills as well as interpersonal skills. I would welcome the opportunity to be a part of your team.

저는 이전 직장 경험을 통해 귀사의 평가에 부합하는 수준 높은 서비스 기술을 습득했습니다. 제 능력이 이 자리에서 귀사가 찾고 있는 것과 완벽하게 어울릴 것 같다고 생각합니다. 이 밖에도, 저는 사람들과 어울려서 일을 잘하고 대인관계 능력 뿐만 아니라 팀워크 능력도 뛰어납니다. 귀사의 팀원이 될 수 있는 기회를 환영합니다.

R3 I consider myself as a dedicated and positive person. Having a positive and determination mind set, I have always believed that anything is possible. During my college days, I was able to obtain academic scholarships for three years consecutively while working in the service industry and volunteering. You should hire me because I believe these qualities will be strong assets to your company. If I am hired, I will utilize my positive attitude and dedication to achieve the company's goals.

저는 제 자신을 헌신적이고 긍정적인 사람으로 여깁니다. 긍정적이고 결단력 있는 마음을 가진 저는 항상 어떤 것이든 가능하다고 믿어 왔습니다. 대학교에 다니는 동안 서비스 업계에서 일을 하고 자원봉사를 하면서도 3년 연속으로 장학금을 받을 수 있었습니다. 저는 이런 자질들이 귀사에 강력한 자산이 될 것이라고 믿기 때문에 저를 채용하셔야 합니다. 만약 제가 채용이 된다면 회사의 목표를 달성하기 위하여 적극적인 태도를 가지고 헌신을 다할 것입니다.

Your Response: 당신의 대답

> ## Key words and expressions · 핵심 단어와 표현

I consider myself as a (descriptive adjective word) person.

저는 제 자신을 (서술적 형용사) 사람이라고 생각합니다.

I am a (descriptive adjective word) person.

저는 (서술적 형용사) 한 사람입니다.

I am very _____ and _____ (use descriptive adjective words).

저는 매우 _____하고 _____ 합니다. (서술적 형용사 사용)

I see myself as a _____ person.

저는 제 자신을 _____ 사람으로 봅니다.

I have obtained (interpersonal/service/problem-solving) skills from my previous job experience.

저는 이전 직장 경험을 통해 (대인관계 기술/서비스 기술/문제 해결) 능력을 얻었습니다.

Grammar Tips 문법 팁 ●

Use 'a' before an adjective with a consonant or a consonant sound.
자음이나 자음의 소리를 가지는 모음이 있는 형용사 앞에 'a'를 사용하라.
Ex: I think of myself as a diligent person.
저는 제 자신을 성실한 사람이라고 생각합니다.

Use 'an' before an adjective with a vowel sound.
모음의 소리가 있는 형용사 앞에는 'an'을 사용하라.
Ex: I consider myself as an energetic person.
저는 제 자신을 활동적인 사람이라고 생각합니다.

Use a reflexive pronoun when the subject and object are the same.
주어와 목적어가 동일한 경우에는 재귀대명사를 사용하라
Ex: I think of myself as a dedicated person.
저는 제 자신을 헌신적인 사람으로 생각합니다.
NOT: I think of me (wrong) as a dedicated person.

Q.3 Why do you want to work here?
당신은 왜 우리 회사에서 일하기를 원합니까?

R1 I have always admired your company because it is one of the most reputable companies in Korea. Your company has a very strong reputation and a positive image with its customers. In recent years, your company has even earned international awards for providing excellent service to its customers. I would like to use my service skills I gained from my educational and work experience to make a positive contribution to your company.

저는 귀하의 회사가 한국에서 가장 명성이 좋은 회사 중 하나이기 때문에 항상 존경해 왔습니다. 귀하의 회사는 고객들로 부터 매우 높은 명성과 긍정적인 이미지를 가지고 있습니다. 최근 몇년 동안에는, 귀하의 회사는 고객들에게 훌륭한 서비스를 제공한 것으로 인해 국제적인 상을 받기도 하였습니다. 저는 제 교육적 경험과 업무 경험에서 얻은 서비스 기술을 사용하여 귀하의 회사에 긍정적인 기여를 하고 싶습니다.

R2 It has always been my dream to become a flight attendant. And to work for a reputable company as yours would be my great achievement.

항공 승무원이 되는 것은 항상 저의 꿈이었습니다. 명성 높은 귀하의 회사에서 일하게 된다면 그것은 저의 위대한 업적이 될 것입니다.

R3 It is important for me to work for a company that values commitment, growth, and diversity. Your company is known to have a long history of doing good work in the community and valuing diversity. It would be my honor to work for a company with such qualities.

저에게는 전념할 수 있고, 발전과 다양성을 중시하는 회사에서 일하는 것이 중요합니다. 귀하의 회사는 지역사회 공헌을 하고 다양성을 가치롭게 여기는 오랜 역사를 지니고 있는 것으로 알려져 있습니다. 그러한 품격을 지닌 회사에서 일하는 것은 저에게 명예로운 일일 것입니다.

Your Response: 당신의 대답

Why do you want to work for us? This is probably one of the most frequent questions that interviewers ask their interviewees. Many employers ask this question to find out which candidates truly want to invest their time to make contributions to the company or they just simply want a job. Take time to research the companies to find out their goals, missions, or benefits of working for them. If their missions or objectives align with the goals of your own, it would be wise to include that in your responses. The key is to demonstrate that you want to be a part of the company to make positive contributions.

왜 우리 회사에서 일하기를 원하십니까? 이 질문은 아마도 면접관들이 인터뷰 대상자에게 가장 자주 묻는 질문 중 하나일 것이다. 많은 고용주들은 이 질문을 통하여 어떤 지원자들이 진정으로 회사에 공헌하기 위해 시간을 투자하고 싶어 하는지 아니면 단순히 일자리를 원하는 것인지를 알기 위하여 이러한 질문을 한다. 면접에 임하기 전에, 회사를 조사하여 회사가 추구하는 직무상의 목표, 임무 혹은 회사의 유익들이 무엇인지 사전 조사해 보아야한다. 조사해 본 회사의 임무나 목표가 자신의 목표와 부합한다면, 그것을 당신의 답변에 포함시키는 것이 좋다. 중요한 것은 당신이 회사의 일원이 되어 긍정적인 기여를 하고 싶다는 것을 입증하는 것이다.

Q.4 **Where do you see yourself in five years?**
당신은 5년 후 어떤 모습으로 있기를 원합니까?

R1 In five years, I would like to be a top performing employee of a leading company in the _____ industry as your company. I hope that I will be considered a valuable employee of _____ taking on more responsibilities and contributing as much as I can.

저는 5년 후에 _____ 업계를 선도하는 회사에서 최고의 실적을 올리는 직원이 되고 싶습니다. _____ 에서 보다 많은 책임을 지고 최대한 많은 공헌을 할 수 있는 가치있는 직원으로 인정 받기를 바랍니다.

R2 In five years, I hope to have moved on from an entry-level service position to a supervision position where I can provide training to new entry-level employees. I think it is important to take on more responsibilities and challenges where I can continue to grow and learn.

저는 5년 후에 일반사원 서비스 직책에서 신입 사원들을 대상으로 교육할 수 있는 감독 분야로 직위를 이동하기를 원합니다. 저는 지속적으로 발전하고 배울 수 있는 더 많은 책임과 도전을 갖는 것이 중요하다고 생각합니다.

R3 I know that your company provides professional development for its employees, so I hope to take advantage of it. It is important that I continue to grow as a valuable employee of your company. In five years, I hope that I have made positive contributions to your company.

귀사가 직원들을 위해 전문적인 개발 서비스를 제공하고 있다는 것을 알고 있기 때문에, 저는 그런 서비스를 이용하기를 소망합니다. 제가 귀사의 가치있는 직원으로 계속 성장하는 것은 중요합니다. 5년 안에 제가 귀사에 긍정적인 공헌을 하기를 바랍니다.

Your Response: 당신의 대답

Key words and expressions • 핵심 단어와 표현

In five years, I would like to be a top performing flight attendant of your airline.

저는 5년 후에는 귀사에서 최고의 항공 승무원이 되고 싶습니다.

In five years, I would like to be working for your airline as a team leader.

5년 후에는 귀하의 항공사에서 팀의 리더로써 일하고 싶습니다.

In five years, I hope I will be a respected role model who trains new employees.

5년 후에, 나는 새로운 직원들을 훈련시키는 존경 받는 롤모델이 되기를 바랍니다.

Q.5 Do you have any questions for us?

우리에게 질문이 있습니까?

R1 Yes. Being a flight attendant with _____ company, what is a typical career path for someone with my skills and experiences? What are the prospects for growth and advancement in this position?

네 있습니다. _____ 회사의 항공 승무원으로서 저의 기술과 경험을 가진 사람에게 전형적인 진로는 무엇입니까? 이 직책에서의 성장과 승진에 대한 전망은 어떻습니까?

R2 Yes. Can you share more about the day-to-day responsibilities of this position? How would you describe a typical day and week in this position?

네 있습니다. 이 직책에서의 일상적인 업무에 대해 좀 더 말씀해 주실 수 있습니까? 이 직책에서의 전형적인 일과와 주간업무를 어떻게 설명하시겠습니까?

R3 Yes, I do. What is the company organization and management style like? How would you describe this company's values?

네, 그렇습니다. 이 회사의 조직과 경영 방식은 어떤가요? 이 회사의 가치를 어떻게 설명하시겠습니까?

R4 What is the most important thing I should accomplish in my first month (the first ninety days)?

첫 달(처음 90일)에 달성해야 할 가장 중요한 일은 무엇입니까?

R5 Can you share some of the challenges of this job? Is there support system to help with these challenges?

이 직업의 어려운 과제들 중 몇 가지를 공유할 수 있나요? 이러한 어려운 과제를 해결하는 데 도움이 되는 지원 시스템이 있습니까?

🖥 Interview Tips 면접 팁 ·

At the end of a job interview, most employers ask prospective employees whether they have any questions. Asking questions can demonstrate that you are well prepared and very energetic to work for the company. Impress your prospective employers by having a list of questions that can illustrate your knowledge and interest in the industry.

입사 면접이 끝나면 대부분의 고용주들은 채용 지원자에게 질문이 있는지 여부를 묻는다. 질문을 하는 것은 당신이 철저히 준비되어 있는 사람이며 회사에서 일하기에 매우 열정적인 사람이라는 것을 보여 줄 수 있다. 업계에 대한 당신의 지식과 관심을 설명해 줄 수 있는 질문 목록을 작성하여 고용주에게 잠재적인 깊은 인상을 줄 수 있도록 해라.

Your Response: 당신의 대답

Let's Practice English • 영어를 연습해 보자

Activity 1: Reading/Writing/Speaking 읽기/쓰기/말하기

Use the following helping verbs to create sentences and/or questions. Share your sentences or questions with your partner.

아래의 조동사를 사용하여 문장이나 질문을 만들어 보고 당신의 문장이나 질문을 당신의 파트너와 서로 공유해 보아라.

1. be (including am, is, are, was, were, been)
2. have, has, had
3. do, does, did
4. can
5. could
6. may
7. might
8. will
9. would
10. shall
11. should
12. must
13. ought to

Your Response: 당신의 대답

Activity 2: Listening/Speaking 듣기/말하기

Role-play with a partner. Have students take turns becoming an interviewer and an interviewee. Use the questions in the chapter to ask and to respond to the questions.

파트너와 함께 role-play를 하시오. 학생들을 면접관과 인터뷰 진행자가 되게 합니다. 이 장의 질문을 사용하여 질문을 하고 질문에 답하시오.

Q.1 Tell me briefly about yourself.
자신에 대하여 간단하게 말해 보세요.

Q.2 Why should we hire you?
왜 우리가 당신을 고용해야 하나요?

Q.3 Why do you want to work here?
당신은 왜 우리 회사에서 일하기를 원합니까?

Q.4 Where do you see yourself in five years?
당신은 5년 후 어떤 모습으로 있기를 원합니까?

Q.5 Do you have any questions for us?
우리에게 질문이 있습니까?

Success in English Interview for Cabin Crew: How to Win the Job Interview

항공 승무원을 위한 성공 영어 인터뷰:
면접에서 승리하는 방법

Chapter 05

Cabin Crew English Interview
Questions

항공 승무원을 위한
영어 면접 질문

Chapter 05

Cabin Crew English Interview Questions
항공 승무원을 위한 영어 면접 질문

Chapter Goals 챕터 목표

✷ To use appropriate expressions to talk about the main duties of cabin crew

적절한 표현을 사용하여 항공 승무원의 주요 업무에 대하여 이야기하기

✷ To use appropriate expressions to talk about the important skills required by cabin crew

적절한 표현을 사용하여 항공 승무원에게 요구되는 중요한 기술에 대해 이야기하기

✷ To practice responding to different interview questions related to the job of cabin crew

항공 승무원의 직무와 관련된 다양한 면접 질문에 대한 답변 연습하기

Grammar Points 핵심 문법

Nouns 명사

Singular nouns are words to illustrate that there is one person, one place, one thing, or one idea. When one single noun or pronoun is associated with the subject of a sentence, the verb needs to agree with the part of the subject. Ex: My hobby is reading books.

단수 명사는 한 사람, 한 곳의 장소, 한 가지 물건, 혹은 한 가지 아이디어가 있음을 설명하는 단어이다. 하나의 명사 또는 대명사가 문장의 주제와 관련이 되어 있을 때, 동사는 주어의 일부와 일치해야 한다. 예시: 나의 취미는 독서이다.

Plural nouns are words to illustrate that there is more than one person, one place, one thing, or one idea. When two or more nouns or pronouns are associated with the subject of a sentence, the verb needs to agree with the part of the subject. Ex: My hobbies are reading books and jogging on weekends.

복수 명사는 한 명 이상의 사람, 한 군데 이상의 장소, 한 개 이상의 물건, 또는 한 개 이상의 아이디어가 있음을 나타내는 단어이다. 두 개 이상의 명사 또는 대명사가 문장의 주제와 관련되어 있을 때 동사는 주제의 일부와 일치해야 한다. 예시: 나의 취미는 주말에 독서와 조깅을 하는 것이다.

 ## Key Vocabulary 주요 어휘

ensure	in charge of	regardless
perform	unexpected	pride
irritable	professionalism	possess
combination	exceptional	committed
obtain	first aid	achieve

 ## Key Expressions 핵심 표현

See each section for key expressions.

각 부분에서 핵심 표현을 참조하라.

🖥 **Interview Tips** 면접 팁 •

When responding to interview questions related to the job of cabin crew and the important skills it requires, it will be helpful to review the job descriptions indicated by the airline companies. Mention the skills or experiences you have that match with what the companies are looking for.

항공 승무원의 업무와 관련된 면접 질문과 이에 필요한 중요한 기술에 대해 답변할 때, 항공사가 제시하는 직무기술서를 검토하는 것이 도움이 될 것이다. 회사가 찾고 있는 것과 일치하는 기술이나 경험을 언급하라.

👤 **Interview Questions**
👥 면접 질문

Q.1 What do you know about the duties of cabin crew members?
항공 승무원의 의무에 대해 무엇을 알고 있습니까?

Q.2 What are the important skills required by cabin crew members?
항공 승무원에게 요구되는 중요한 기술은 무엇입니까?

Q.3 Why do you want to become a cabin crew?
왜 항공 승무원이 되기를 원합니까?

Q.4 What are some advantages and disadvantages of being a cabin crew?
승무원 직업의 장점과 단점은 무엇입니까?

Q.5 Does your personality suit the job of a cabin crew?
당신의 성격이 항공 승무원의 직업에 적절한가요?

Interview Questions & Sample Responses
면접 질문 및 응답 샘플

Q.1 What do you know about the duties of cabin crew members?

항공 승무원의 의무에 대해 무엇을 알고 있습니까?

R1 There are many responsibilities of cabin crew members. However, the main duties of a cabin crew are to provide excellent in-flight service while ensuring the safety and comfort of airline passengers. For example, flight attendants are responsible for directing airline passengers in case of emergencies and providing first aid when necessary. They also need to provide service such as serving meals and refreshments and selling duty-free goods.

항공 승무원들에게는 많은 책임이 있습니다. 하지만 항공 승무원들의 주요 임무는 훌륭한 기내 서비스를 제공하는 동시에 승객들의 안전과 편의를 보장하는 것입니다. 예를 들어, 항공 승무원들은 응급 상황이 발생한 경우 승객을 안내하고 필요한 경우 응급 처치를 제공해야 합니다. 그들은 또한 식사와 다과를 제공하고 면세품을 판매하는 것과 같은 서비스도 제공하여야 합니다.

R2 Cabin crews are in charge of providing customer service to airline passengers throughout the flight. Their main priorities are to provide pleasant flying experience and to meet the needs of airline passengers. Some of the duties include guiding passengers to their seats, helping them with their carry-on luggage, serving them with meals and refreshments, and providing emergency directions when necessary.

항공 승무원은 비행 중에 승객들에게 고객서비스를 제공하는 역할을 담당합니다. 주요 우선순위는 쾌적한 비행 경험을 제공하고 승객들의 요구를 충족시키는 것입니다. 이러한 임무 중에는 승객을 좌석으로 안내하고, 기내 반입 수하물을 들어 주고, 식사와 다과를 제공하며, 필요한 경우 비상 상황시 안내를 제공하는 일이 포함되어 있습니다.

R3 There are many different roles of cabin crew members. However, one of the most important responsibilities is to provide pleasant service so that passengers travel comfortably and safely.

항공 승무원의 역할에는 여러가지가 있습니다. 그러나 가장 중요한 책임 중 하나는 승객이 편안하고 안전하게 여행 할 수 있도록 쾌적한 서비스를 제공하는 것입니다.

Your Response: 당신의 대답

Q.2 What are the important skills required by cabin crew members?
항공 승무원에게 요구되는 중요한 기술은 무엇입니까?

R1 I believe that it is important for cabin crew members to have good communication skills. Since they interact with people from different backgrounds and cultures, flight attendants need to have good communication skills in order to meet the needs of various passengers. Flight attendants also need to be flexible and patient as their job is to make passengers feel comfortable and pleasant.

항공 승무원들은 훌륭한 의사소통 기술을 갖는 것이 중요하다고 생각합니다. 그들은 서로 다른 배경과 문화에서 온 사람들과 상호 작용을 하기 때문에, 항공 승무원들은 다양한 승객들의 요구를 충족시키기 위해서 훌륭한 의사소통 기술을 가져야 합니다. 또한 항공 승무원들은 유연해야 하고 인내심을 가질 필요가 있는데 그들의 일이 승객들을 편안하고 즐겁게 해 주는 것이기 때문입니다.

R2 The important skills for cabin crew members are effective teamwork and interpersonal skills. Most often cabin crew members work with different team members and they also have different duties while on the job. Therefore, in order to ensure all duties are performed in a right way, all involved members should be good team players. Having good interpersonal skills helps when doing teamwork.

항공 승무원들에게 중요한 기술은 효율적인 팀워크와 대인관계 능력입니다. 대부분의 항공 승무원들은 다른 팀원들과 함께 일하고 또한 근무 중에 다른 업무를 수행합니다. 따라서 모든 임무가 올바르게 수행되도록 하기 위해서, 관련된 모든 구성원들은 효율적인 팀원이 되어야 합니다. 훌륭한 대인관계 기술을 갖는 것은 팀워크를 수행할 때 도움이 됩니다.

R3 I believe that flight attendants should have excellent people skills. This means that flight attendants should always be polite and professional to all passengers regardless of their moods.

It is flight attendants' job to provide excellent service and to demonstrate their professionalism through their actions even if they are dealing with difficult customers.

저는 항공 승무원들이 뛰어난 대인관계 기술을 가져야 한다고 믿습니다. 이것은 항공 승무원들이 자신들의 기분과 상관없이 모든 승객들에게 언제나 공손하고 전문적이어야 한다는 것을 의미합니다. 까다로운 고객을 상대하고 있더라도 훌륭한 서비스를 제공하고 그들의 행동을 통해 전문성을 보여 주는 것이 항공 승무원들의 업무이기 때문입니다.

Your Response: 당신의 대답

📷 Interview Tips 면접 팁 •••••••••••••••••••••••••••••

Some of the qualities that many airlines look for in their hiring recruits are exceptional customer service, confidence, flexibility, adaptability, cultural awareness, teamwork and communication skills.

많은 항공사들이 신입 사원을 채용할 때 요구하는 자질은 탁월한 고객 서비스, 자신감, 유연성, 적응력, 문화적 인식, 팀워크 및 의사소통 능력 등이 있다.

Q.3 Why do you want to become a cabin crew?

왜 항공 승무원이 되기를 원합니까?

R1 It has always been my dream to become a flight attendant. I enjoy working with people, and I particularly like meeting people from all over the world.

항공 승무원이 되는 것이 항상 저의 꿈이었습니다. 저는 사람들과 일하는 것을 즐기고, 특히 전 세계 사람들을 만나는 것을 좋아합니다.

R2 I have always enjoyed my part-time jobs working in the service industry. That is one of the reasons why I pursued a degree in airline services. I want to become a flight attendant because I enjoy providing good quality service to customers. Being a flight attendant, I will also have pride in my work.

저는 항상 서비스업에서 일하는 아르바이트를 즐겨 왔습니다. 이것이 제가 항공 서비스 분야에서 학위를 취득한 이유 중 하나입니다. 저는 고객들에게 양질의 서비스를 제공하는 것을 좋아하기 때문에 항공 승무원이 되고 싶습니다. 또한 항공 승무원의 직업은 저에게 자부심을 줄 것입니다.

R3 I have always enjoyed traveling and learning about different cultures. As a result, I have been to many different places and met various people from all over the world. Being a flight attendant, I will always be doing what I enjoy the most.

저는 항상 여행하는 것, 그리고 다른 문화에 대해 배우는 것을 즐겨 왔습니다. 그 결과, 저는 다양한 많은 곳들을 다녔고 전 세계의 다양한 사람들을 만났습니다. 승무원이 되면, 언제나 제가 가장 즐기는 일을 할 것이기 때문입니다.

Your Response: 당신의 대답

(Q.4) What are some advantages and disadvantages of being a cabin crew?

승무원 직업의 장점과 단점은 무엇입니까?

(R1) I believe there are lots of advantages of being a cabin crew. One of the main advantages is that there are many opportunities to travel and to experience different cultures and customs. Another big advantage is that flight attendants can meet people from all over the world. I certainly believe that there are more advantages than disadvantages of being a flight attendant. But one main disadvantage is that this line of work requires long working hours. Also, traveling long hours can be tiring if one is not in good health condition. So, it is wise to be in good shape to work as a flight attendant.

저는 항공 승무원의 일에 많은 장점들이 있다고 믿습니다. 주요 장점 중 하나는 여행을 하며 다양한 문화와 관습을 경험할 수 있는 기회가 많다는 것입니다. 또 다른 큰 장점은 항공 승무원들이 전 세계 사람들을 만날 수 있다는 것입니다. 저는 확실히 이 직업에선 단점보다 더 많은 장점이 있다고 믿습니다. 그러나 한 가지 주요 단점은 이 직업은 긴 근무 시간을 필요로 한다는 것입니다. 또한 만약 사람이 건강하지 않다면 긴 시간 여행하는 것도 피곤할 수 있습니다. 그래서 승무원으로 일하기 위해서 좋은 건강 상태를 유지하는 것이 현명합니다.

R2 Some advantages of this line of work are that flight attendants work with various people and work in teams. Since they work with all kinds of people and do lots of teamwork, they will have opportunities to meet lots of people. And doing teamwork can also make their work more interesting and manageable. But if people do not enjoy doing teamwork, this can be a disadvantage. Also not all people they meet can be friendly, so sometimes flight attendants can work with people, including customers and colleagues, who are difficult and irritable.

이 직종의 장점 중 하나는 항공 승무원들이 다양한 사람들과 함께 팀으로 일한다는 것입니다. 그들은 다양한 사람들과 함께 일하며 팀워크를 해야하기 때문에, 많은 사람들을 만날 기회를 가질 것입니다. 그리고 팀워크를 통해 그들의 일을 좀 더 흥미롭게 하고 업무를 처리하기 쉽게 만들 수 있습니다. 하지만 만약 사람들이 팀워크를 즐기지 않는다면, 이것은 단점이 될 수 있습니다. 또한 그들이 만나는 모든 사람들이 친절할 수 있는 것은 아니기 때문에 상황에 따라 항공 승무원들은 까다롭고 예민한 사람들과 함께 일할 수도 있습니다.

(R3) This line of work allows flight attendants to experience and to visit many different countries. Also being in this line of work provides travel benefits and flexible days off. One main disadvantage is that flight attendants can experience unexpected situations. These unexpected situations can be minor situations but also serious and dangerous ones.

이 업무를 통해 다른 나라를 경험하고 방문 할 수 있습니다. 또한 이 직업은 여행의 혜택과 유연한 휴가를 제공합니다. 이 업무의 주요 단점 중 하나는 예기치 못한 상황을 경험할 수 있다는 것입니다. 이러한 예기치 않은 상황은 경미한 상황일 수도 있지만 심각하고 위험한 상황일 수도 있습니다.

Your Response: 당신의 대답

> **Key words and expressions •** 핵심 단어와 표현

Advantages of being a cabin crew 항공 승무원 직업의 장점

Flight attendants have opportunities to ⋯⋯

항공 승무원들은 _____ 할 수 있는 기회가 있습니다.

- ☑ Travel different countries
  여러 나라를 여행

- ☑ Experience various cultures and customs
  다양한 문화와 풍습 체험

- ☑ Meet people from all over the world
  전 세계에서 온 사람들을 만날 수

- ☑ Experience the local life while working
  근무하는 동안에 현지 생활을 경험

- ☑ Work with various people with different backgrounds
  다양한 배경을 지닌 다양한 사람들과의 협력

- ☑ Work in teams and do teamwork
  팀으로 일하고 팀워크를 활용

- ☑ Wear unique and professional uniform to work
  근무 시 회사 고유의 전문적인 유니폼 착용

- ☑ Work different working hours
  근무 시간이 다른 시간에 근무

- ☑ Obtain travel benefits for employees and their family
  직원 및 직원 가족의 출장 수당 획득

- ☑ Gain excellent service and interpersonal skills
  뛰어난 서비스 및 대인관계 능력 확보

Disadvantages of being a cabin crew 항공 승무원 직업의 단점

Flight attendants .....

항공 승무원들은 _____

☑ work long hours (sometimes 12-15 hour shifts) and experience jet lag
장시간 (때로는 12-15시간 교대) 근무 및 시차로 인한 피로 경험함

☑ can experience unexpected and dangerous situations
예기치 못하고 위험한 상황을 겪을 수 있음

☑ can work with difficult passengers and crew members
까다로운 탑승자 및 항공 승무원과도 협력 가능

☑ can miss family and holiday gatherings due to different work schedule
근무 시간이 달라 가족 및 휴일 모임을 놓칠 수 있음

☑ do not have regular work schedule
정기적인 근무 일정이 없음

Q.5 Does your personality suit the job of a cabin crew?
당신의 성격이 항공 승무원의 직업에 적절한가요?

R1 I definitely believe my personality suits the job of a cabin crew. I am very attentive and observant. These traits are essential for flight attendants because they need to understand their passengers to provide the best service for them. I also believe these qualities help when working with other crew team members.

저는 제 성격이 항공 승무원의 직업에 꼭 맞는다고 생각합니다. 저는 제가 매우 세심하고 주의 깊다고 생각합니다. 이러한 특성들은 최상의 서비스를 제공하기 위해 그들의 승객들을 이해할 필요가 있기 때문에 항공 승무원들에게 필수적입니다. 저는 또한 이러한 자질들이 다른 항공 승무원 팀 구성원들과 협력 할 때 도움이 된다고 믿습니다.

R2 Absolutely! I am very open-minded and adaptable. I respect different people's perspectives and enjoy learning new things. Because of this nature, I like challenges and enjoy finding ways to make things better.

물론입니다! 저는 매우 개방적이고 적응력이 좋습니다. 저는 다른 사람들의 관점을 존중하고 새로운 것을 배우는 것을 즐깁니다. 이런 성격 때문에 저는 도전을 좋아하며 일하는데 더 좋은 방법을 찾는 것을 즐깁니다.

R3 Yes, I consider myself as a positive and calm person. So even if I encounter challenges, I think very positively about them. I also have a tendency to stay calm under pressure or stressful situations. Flight attendants often face unexpected situations during flights, so these traits will be useful when I work as a flight attendant.

예, 저는 제 자신을 긍정적이고 침착한 사람으로 생각합니다. 그래서 도전에 직면하더라도, 저는 그것들에 대해 매우 긍정적으로 생각합니다. 저는 또한 압박감이나 스트레스가 많은 상황에서 침착함을 유지하는 경향이 있습니다. 항공 승무원은 종종 비행 중에 예기치 않은 상황에 직면하기 때문에 항공 승무원으로 일하는 경우 이러한 자질이 유용할 것입니다.

📖 Interview Tips 면접 팁 •

Respond positively and confidently with this interview question. Use this question to demonstrate your strengths!

이 면접의 질문에 긍정적이고 자신 있게 답변해야 한다. 이 질문을 사용하여 당신의 장점을 입증하라.

Your Response: 당신의 대답

Let's Practice English • 영어를 연습해 보자

Activity 1: Writing/Speaking 쓰기/말하기

Write down some of the duties of a flight attendant in complete sentences.
Share them with your partner.

항공 승무원의 의무를 완전한 문장으로 작성하고 파트너와 공유하라.

Activity 2: Writing/Speaking 쓰기/말하기

What are some of the essential skills that flight attendants should have?
Write them down and share them with your partner. Ask whether they agree
with you.

항공 승무원들이 갖춰야 할 필수적인 기술에는 어떤 것들이 있을까? 그것들을 적어서
파트너와 나누어 보아라. 그들이 당신에게 동의하는지 물어보아라.

Example: communication skills 의사소통 기술

A: I think that flight attendants should have good communication skills.
Do you agree?
저는 항공 승무원들은 의사소통 능력이 좋아야 한다고 생각합니다. 동의합니까?

B: Yes, I agree. Flight attendants work with so many diverse people,
so it is important to have good communication skills.
맞습니다. 저도 그렇게 생각합니다. 항공 승무원들은 아주 많은 다양한 사람들과 함께 일
을 합니다. 그래서 좋은 의사소통 기술을 갖는 것은 중요합니다.

Success in English Interview for Cabin Crew: How to Win the Job Interview

항공 승무원을 위한 성공 영어 인터뷰:
면접에서 승리하는 방법

Chapter 06

Strengths and Weaknesses
Interview Questions

강점과 약점 면접 질문

Chapter 06

Strengths and Weaknesses Interview Questions
강점과 약점 면접 질문

Chapter Goals 챕터 목표

- To use appropriate expressions to talk about your strengths
  적절한 표현을 사용하여 자신의 강점에 대해 이야기하기
- To use appropriate expressions to talk about your weaknesses
  적절한 표현을 사용하여 자신의 약점에 대해 이야기하기
- To practice responding to different interview questions about strengths and weaknesses
  강점과 약점의 다양한 면접 질문에 대한 답변 연습하기

Grammar Points 핵심 문법

Adjective and Verb Placement 형용사와 동사 배치

An adjective describes a person, a place, or a thing. Adjectives are usually placed before nouns they modify. However, when used with linking verbs, such as forms of 'to be' and 'sense verbs', they are placed after the verb. Use adverb words such as very and extremely before adjectives to make adjectives stronger.

형용사는 사람, 장소 또는 사물을 묘사한다. 형용사는 일반적으로 명사 앞에 위치한다. 그러나 'to be' 그리고 'sense verbs'와 같은 연결 동사(예: look, remain, seem)와 함께 사용될 때는 동사 뒤에 배치된다. 형용사를 강하게 만들 때 '매우, 극단적으로' 와 같은 부사를 형용사 앞에 사용하라.

 ## Key Vocabulary 주요 어휘

previous	mediocre	blunt
suitable	require	task
diverse	priority	pride
encourage	appropriate	excel
specific	uptight	loosen up

 ## Key Expressions 핵심 표현

See each section for key expressions.

각 부분에서 핵심 표현을 참조하자.

🖥️ Interview Tips 면접 팁 •

Asking job candidates to talk about their strengths and weaknesses is perhaps one of the most common questions during job interviews. Regardless of the different job positions, almost all prospective employers often ask candidates to discuss their strengths and/or weaknesses. How candidates respond to this question will have a big impact on their chances of getting hired or perhaps not getting hired. Prospective employers use candidates' responses to determine if they are the right fit for the position and for the company as well as the challenges they could encounter if the candidates are hired.

입사 지원자에게 자신의 장점과 단점에 대해 이야기하도록 요구하는 것은 아마도 면접 중에 가장 자주 제기되는 질문 중 하나일 것이다. 각기 다른 직책에 관계없이 거의 모든 예비 고용주는 지원자에게 강점과 약점에 대해 논의하도록 요청한다. 이 질문에 대한 지원자들의 답변은 그들이 채용되거나 채용되지 않을 가능성에 큰 영향을 미칠 것이다. 예비 고용주는 지원자의 대답을 듣고 지원자들이 직책과 회사에 적합한지를 보고 또 지원자들이 고용될 때 발생할 수 있는 어려움들을 판단한다.

Use the following tips when responding to questions related to strengths and weaknesses
장점과 단점이 관련된 질문에 대답 할 때 다음 팁을 사용하라

Keep your responses related to strengths and weaknesses to job, school, or volunteer experience.

직장, 학교, 혹은 자원 봉사 경험과 관련된 강점과 약점에 관한 대답을 지속한다.

Do not be humble with your strengths. You need to be the key advocate for yourself.

당신의 강점에 대해서 겸손하지 마라. 당신은 자신을 위한 주요 지지자가 되어야한다.

Select the strengths that are most applicable to the job.

직업에 가장 적합한 강점을 선택하라.

Minimize weaknesses that could be problematic for the job. For example, if the job requires a lot of teamwork, but your weakness is working with people, that could make you unfit for the job.

직업에 문제가 될 수 있는 약점을 최소화하라. 예를 들어 업무에 많은 팀워크가 필요하지만 당신의 약점이 다른 사람과 일하는 것이라면 그것이 당신을 그 직업에 맞지 않게 만들 수 있다.

When talking about your weakness, always talk about how you handle your weakness.

약점에 대해 이야기 할 때는, 당신이 당신의 약점을 어떻게 관리하는지에 대하여 항상 이야기 하라.

Interview Questions
면접 질문

Q.1 What is your greatest strength? What are your greatest strengths?
당신의 가장 큰 강점은 무엇입니까?

Q.2 Why are you the best person for the job?
Why should we choose you for the job?

왜 당신이 이 직업에 가장 적합한 사람이라고 생각합니까?
이 직업에 왜 우리가 당신을 선택해야 합니까?

Q.3 What is your greatest weakness? What are your weaknesses?
당신의 가장 큰 약점은 무엇입니까?

Q.4 What would you want to change about your personality?
당신의 성격에 관해 무엇을 바꾸고 싶습니까?

Q.5 What motivates you in life?
무엇이 당신의 삶에 동기를 부여합니까?

Words to Describe Positive Personality Traits
긍정적인 성격을 나타내는 단어

- ☑ adaptable – 적응을 잘하는
- ☑ easygoing – 느긋한, 소탈한
- ☑ approachable – 친근한
- ☑ energetic – 활기가 넘치는, 열광적인
- ☑ ambitious – 야망있는
- ☑ enthusiastic/passionate – 열정적인
- ☑ active – 활동적인
- ☑ friendly – 친절한, 다정스러운
- ☑ attentive – 주의를 살피는, 배려하는
- ☑ flexible – 융통성이 있는
- ☑ amiable – 정감있는
- ☑ independent – 독립적인
- ☑ calm – 차분한
- ☑ open-minded– 개방적인, 마음이 열려있는
- ☑ committed/dedicated – 헌신적인
- ☑ organized – 정리를 잘하는, 체계적인
- ☑ compassionate/caring – 인정 많은
- ☑ polite – 공손한, 정중한
- ☑ cheerful – 쾌활한, 발랄한
- ☑ patient – 인내심이 강한
- ☑ cooperative – 협조적인
- ☑ reliable/trustworthy – 믿을 수 있는
- ☑ creative/imaginative – 창의력이 있는
- ☑ thoughtful/understanding – 배려 깊은
- ☑ diligent/hardworking – 성실한, 근면한
- ☑ sociable/outgoing – 사교 적인, 외향적인
- ☑ determined – 결심한
- ☑ warm-hearted – 마음이 따듯한
- ☑ sensible – 똑똑한
- ☑ decisive – 결단력이 있는

☑ sincere – 성실한
☑ witty/resourceful/clever – 재치있는
☑ confident – 자신감 있는
☑ perceptive – 지각있는
☑ generous – 관대한, 너그러운
☑ punctual – 시간을 잘 지키는
☑ devoted – 헌신적인
☑ bright – 똑똑한
☑ humorous – 재미있는
☑ insightful – 통찰력 있는
☑ responsible – 책임감이 강한
☑ positive – 긍정적인

 Words to Describe Negative Personality Traits
부정적인 성격을 나타내는 단어

☑ uptight – 불안해하는
☑ careless – 조심성이 없는
☑ negative – 부정적인
☑ indecisive – 우유부단한
☑ close-minded – 고지식한
☑ demanding – 요구가 많은
☑ self-centered – 자기중심적인
☑ perfectionist – 완벽 주의자
☑ emotional – 감성적인
☑ blunt/direct – 직선적인
☑ impatient – 참을성이 없는
☑ skeptical –의심 많은
☑ impulsive – 충동적인
☑ opinionated – 완고한

Interview Questions & Sample Responses
면접 질문 및 응답 샘플

Q.1 What is your greatest strength? What are your greatest strengths?
당신의 가장 큰 강점은 무엇입니까?

R1 My greatest strength is that I am energetic. I have always been very passionate about life in general. As a result, I have done well in college. I was also involved in various extra-curricular activities and even took leadership positions. I believe my strength will be helpful when I work as a flight attendant.

저의 가장 큰 강점은 제가 열정적이라는 것입니다. 저는 항상 삶에 대해 매우 열정적 이었습니다. 그 결과 저는 대학생활을 잘 마무리 했습니다. 저는 또한 다양한 동아리 활동에 참여했으며 리더의 위치에 있었습니다. 제가 항공 승무원으로 일할 때 저의 강점이 도움이 될 것이라고 믿습니다.

R2 I believe one of my greatest strengths is that I am diligent and hardworking. Because of this trait, I have received positive comments from my previous employers. I don't believe in mediocre work. I always give my best efforts for everything I do.

저의 가장 큰 강점 중 하나는 제가 근면하고 부지런하다는 것입니다. 이러한 특성으로 인해 저는 이전 고용주로부터 긍정적인 평가를 받았습니다. 저는 평범하게 일을 하는 것을 믿지 않습니다. 저는 항상 최선을 다합니다.

R3 I have a very strong sense of work ethic and responsibility. I feel my greatest strengths are that I am committed and responsible. When I am given a task, I always give my best effort to complete it and complete it well. I have been told by my previous employers that I was a good employee because I was always on time and did more than what was required of me.

저는 매우 강한 직업윤리와 책임감을 가지고 있습니다. 그렇기 때문에 저의 가장 큰 강점은 제가 헌신적이고 책임감이 강하다는 것입니다. 저는 주어진 과제를 잘 완수하기 위해서 항상 최선을 다합니다. 저는 항상 정확한 시간에 출근해서 저에게 요구되는 것보다 더 많은 일들을 했기 때문에 이전 고용주들로 부터 좋은 직원이었다는 말을 들었습니다.

Your Response: 당신의 대답

Key words and expressions • 핵심 단어와 표현

My greatest strength is that I am (descriptive adjective word).

저의 가장 큰 강점은 제가 (서술 형용사) 라는 것입니다.

My main/key strength is my ability to work well with others.

저의 주요 강점은 다른 사람들과 협력을 잘하는 능력입니다.

I have a natural ability to work in a busy environment.

저는 바쁜 환경에서 자연스럽게 일을 할 수 있는 능력을 가지고 있습니다.

One of my greatest strengths is that I am (descriptive adjective word).

저의 가장 큰 강점 중 한 가지는 제가 (서술 형용사) 라는 것입니다.

My strength is that I have a sense of strong work ethic.

저의 강점은 제가 강한 직업윤리 의식을 가지고 있다는 것입니다.

Having excellent _____ skills is my main strength.

뛰어난 _____ 기술을 가진 것이 저의 주요 강점입니다.

I am quite good at remaining calm in a chaotic situation.

저는 혼란스러운 상황에서 침착함을 유지하는 데 꽤 능숙합니다.

I am excellent at teamwork and working with others. (use noun or gerund/-ing)

저는 팀워크가 뛰어나고 다른 사람들과 함께 일하는 것을 매우 잘합니다.

I am excellent/good at

(나는 -------에 뛰어나다)

☑ interacting with team members –팀원들과 상호 작용하는데
☑ organizing paperwork –서류 정리하는 것
☑ managing time –시간 관리하는 것
☑ coordinating team projects –팀 프로젝트 조정하는 것
☑ understanding other people's perspectives. –다른 사람들의 관점을 이해하는데

> **List of Positive and Valuable Traits and Skills for Job Interview**
> 면접을 위한 긍정적이고 가치 있는 표현

☑ ability to work well with others – 다른 사람들과 잘 어울리는 능력
☑ people skills – 대인관계
☑ ability to adapt – 적응 능력
☑ organizational skills – 조직력
☑ ability to remain calm – 침착함을 유지하는 능력
☑ a sense of strong work ethic – 확고한 직장 윤리 의식
☑ strong interpersonal skills – 훌륭한 대인 관계 기술
☑ a sense of professionalism – 전문성 감각
☑ problem-solving skills – 문제 해결 능력
☑ a sense of responsibility – 책임 의식
☑ effective communication skills – 효과적인 의사소통 기술
☑ a sense of leadership – 리더십 감각

Q.2 Why are you the best person for the job?
Why should we choose you for the job?

왜 당신이 이 직업에 가장 적합한 사람이라고 생각합니까?
이 직업에 왜 우리가 당신을 선택해야 합니까?

R1 I am very suitable for the job because I possess a combination of skills and experience that will be useful to work as a flight attendant. I have a degree in airline services and I have more than two years of experience working in the service industry.

저는 승무원으로 일하는데 유용한 기술과 경험을 겸비하고 있기 때문에 그 일에 매우 적합합니다. 저는 항공 서비스 분야에서 학위를 가지고 있고 서비스 업계에서 2년 이상의 경력을 쌓았습니다.

R2 I feel I am the best person for the job because I have excellent interpersonal and teamwork skills. I am very open-minded and enjoy working with many different types of people. The job of a cabin crew requires working with diverse passengers and team crew members, so having good people skills will be very useful.

저는 대인관계 능력과 팀워크 기술이 뛰어나기 때문에 제가 그 일의 적임자라고 생각합니다. 저는 매우 개방적이고 다양한 유형의 사람들과 일하는 것을 즐깁니다. 승무원의 업무는 다양한 승객들과 팀 구성원들이 함께 협력하여 일하는 것을 필요로 하기 때문에, 뛰어난 대인관계 기술을 갖춘 것은 매우 유용할 것입니다.

R3 You should choose me for the job because I am dedicated and committed. I have always taken great pride in all of my work. As a result, when I was a student or when I worked part-time jobs, I have always provided my best performance. If I become your employee, I know I will provide successful results.

이 직업을 위해 저를 선택해야하는 이유는 저는 늘 헌신적이고 항상 노력하기 때문입니다. 저는 항상 제 모든 일에 큰 자부심을 가졌습니다. 그 결과 저는 학생이었을 때나 아르바이트 일을 할 때도 항상 최고의 성적을 제공했습니다. 제가 귀사의 직원이 된다면, 성공적인 결과를 제공할 것을 알고 있습니다.

🖼 Interview Tips 면접 팁 •

Respond confidently to this interview question. Remember you are persuading your interviewer why you are the most suitable person for the job.

이 면접 질문에 자신 있게 대답하라. 당신이 이 직업에 가장 적합한 사람이라는 이유를 면접관에게 설득하는 것을 잊지 마라.

Q.3 What is your greatest weakness? What are your weaknesses?

당신의 가장 큰 약점은 무엇입니까?

R1 Well, I have been called a perfectionist before, so that could be my weakness. Being perfectionist can be very tiring sometimes because it takes too much time to complete any task. It is good to pay attention to details, but it is not healthy to be obsessive with everything. Now I try to focus on the main priorities in each task and move on to other tasks.

음, 저는 전에 완벽주의자라고 불려 왔습니다. 그래서 그것이 저의 약점일 수도 있습니다. 완벽주의자가 되는 것은 어떤 일을 완수하는 데 너무 많은 시간이 걸리기 때문에 때때로 저를 매우 지치게 할 수 있습니다. 세부적인 것에 주의를 기울이는 것은 좋지만, 모든 것에 강박적이 되는 것은 건강에 좋지 않습니다. 이제 저는 각각의 업무에서 주요 우선순위에 초점을 맞추고 다른 업무로 넘어갈 것입니다.

R2 My weakness is that I do not have a lot of job experience. I only worked few part-time jobs. During college years, I wanted to focus on my studies and I participated in many extracurricular activities.

저의 약점은 제가 직장 경험이 많지 않다는 것입니다. 저는 단지 몇 가지의 아르바이트 일만 했습니다. 대학 시절에 저는 공부에 집중하기를 원했고 많은 학교 동아리 활동에 참여하였습니다.

R3 I think that I can be indecisive sometimes. This could be that because I think too much, it just takes too much time to make a decision. Now I try to write down pros and cons with each decision and just select the most appropriate decision based on the positive and negative points.

저는 가끔씩 제가 우유부단 할 수 있다고 생각합니다. 이것은 제가 굉장히 많은 생각을 하기 때문에 결정을 내리는 데 너무 많은 시간이 걸릴 수 있다는 것입니다. 이

제 저는 각 결정에 따라 찬반양론을 기록하고 긍정적인 관점과 부정적인 관점에 기초한 가장 적절한 결정을 선택하려고 합니다.

Your Response: 당신의 대답

(Q.4) **What would you want to change about your personality?**
당신의 성격에 대해 무엇을 바꾸고 싶습니까?

(R1) I wish I could be more assertive. Sometimes I care more about people's feelings, so I have a difficult time sharing how I truly feel about a topic.

저는 더 단호하게 행동할 수 있기를 바랍니다. 가끔 저는 다른 사람들의 감정에 더 신경을 쓰기 때문에 하나의 화제에 대해 진심으로 어떻게 느끼는지를 공유하는데 어려움을 겪습니다.

R2 Well, I have been told that I can be too direct or even blunt sometimes. So I wish to be more sensitive and careful in terms of what I say and how I say things to people.

음, 저는 제가 때때로 너무 무뚝뚝하고 심지어 너무 퉁명스럽다고 들었습니다. 그래서 저는 사람들에게 말하는 방식에 있어서 좀 더 섬세해지고 신중해지고 싶습니다.

R3 I can be uptight sometimes because I tend to worry too much. So I wish I could relax more and not worry so much. Nowadays, I try to loosen up more by thinking postively.

저는 너무 걱정하는 경향이 있기 때문에 때때로 불안해합니다. 그래서 저는 더 많이 편하게 생각하고 너무 걱정하지 않기를 바랍니다. 요즘 저는 긍정적인 사고를 생각함으로써 좀 더 긴장을 풀어내려고 노력하고 있습니다.

Your Response: 당신의 대답

> ### Key words and expressions • 핵심 단어와 표현

I would like to be more _____.

저는 좀 더 _____한 사람이 되고 싶습니다.

I wish I could be _____.

저는 _____한 사람이 되고 싶습니다.

I would want to be more _____.

저는 좀 더 _____한 사람이 되고 싶습니다.

Q.5 What motivates you in life?
무엇이 당신의 삶에 동기를 부여합니까?

R1 I probably motivate myself the most. I have always been motivated to do well in school and at work because it was important to give my best effort in given tasks. Since I had specific goals for going to school and going to work, it was easy for me to be motivated.

저는 제 자신에게 가장 동기를 많이 부여 하는 사람일 것입니다. 저는 주어진 과제에 최선을 다하는 것이 중요했기 때문에 항상 학교에서나 직장에서 잘 하도록 동기를 부여하였습니다. 저는 학교에 다니고 일을 하는 것에 구체적인 목표를 갖고 있었기 때문에 동기부여가 되는 것은 어렵지 않았습니다.

R2 I am motivated because it has always been my dream to become a flight attendant. Having such a dream motivated me to work hard and to always excel in everything I do.

저는 지금까지 항공 승무원이 되는 것이 제 꿈이었기 때문에 그것으로 동기를 부여 받고 있습니다. 그러한 꿈을 가지고 있는 것은 항상 제가 하는 모든 일에 뛰어나도 록 동기부여가 되었습니다.

R3 Perhaps my family motivates me in a positive way. We are strong close-knit family and have always encouraged one another to do well in life. Because of this special relationship, we support one another to do the best in everything.

저의 가족은 긍정적인 방식으로 저에게 동기를 부여하는 것 같습니다. 저희 가족은 강하고 친밀하게 맺어져 항상 서로가 삶을 잘 영위해 나가도록 격려해 왔습니다. 이 러한 특별한 관계로 인하여, 저희 가족은 모든 일에 최선을 다할 수 있도록 서로를 지원합니다.

Your Response: 당신의 대답

Let's Practice English · 영어를 연습해 보자

Activity 1: Listening/Speaking 듣기/말하기

Use the words from this chapter that are used to describe personality traits to ask yes/no questions to your partner.

성격 특성을 묘사 할 때 쓰는 단어를 사용하여 예/아니오 질문을 파트너에게 질문을 하라.

Example

You: Are you decisive?
Your Partner: Not really. Sometimes I think too much, so I am not decisive.

Activity 2: Listening/Speaking 듣기/말하기

Work in a group. One person selects a word from the list below and each person in the group gives one sentence that describes the word.

한 사람이 아래 목록에서 한 단어를 선택하면 그룹의 각 사람이 그 단어를 설명하며 문장을 만든다.

Example

Person 1: Someone who is responsible…

Person 2: She/he is good at work.

Person 3: She/he does work on time.

Person 4: She/he works hard.

Success in English Interview for Cabin Crew: How to Win the Job Interview

항공 승무원을 위한 성공 영어 인터뷰:
면접에서 승리하는 방법

Chapter 07

Difficult Interview Questions
어려운 면접 질문

Chapter 07

Difficult Interview Questions
어려운 면접 질문

 Chapter Goals 챕터 목표

✗ To identify difficult interview questions

어려운 면접 질문을 인식하기

✗ To use appropriate expressions to respond to behavioral interview questions

적절한 표현을 사용하여 행동 면접 질문에 답변하기

 Grammar Points 핵심 문법

Modal Verb: Would

'Would' is a modal auxiliary verb. We use 'would' to mainly express want, polite requests and questions, opinion, or wish. We also use 'would' to talk about the past. The basic structure is subject + auxiliary verb 'would' + main verb. Thus, we can't use 'would' modal verb without a main verb.

'Would'는 조동사 이다. 주로 원하는 것, 정중한 요청, 질문, 의견 또는 소원을 표현하기 위해 'would'를 사용한다. 그리고 또 과거에 대해 이야기하기 위해 'would'를 사용한다. 기본 구조는 주어 + 조동사 'would'+ 주동사 이다. 따라서 주동사 없이 조동사 'would'를 사용할 수 없다.

Key Vocabulary 주요 어휘

resolve	conflicts	identify
reflect	perspective	manner
suffered	attentively	inform
fault	frustration	remedy
unexpected	relate	discuss

Key Expressions 핵심 표현

See each section for key expressions.

각 부분에서 핵심 표현을 참조하라.

Interview Tips 면접 팁 ●

All job interview questions can be tough, but some types of questions can be more difficult. Interviewers do not ask challenging interview questions to find out whether you possess the right answers. They ask challenging questions to find out how you would react to them and to also discern if you are the right fit for their company. Do not panic if some of the interview questions are challenging. Think positive and provide logical responses that perhaps include concrete examples of skills and experience that relate directly to the position. The behavioral interview questions relate to how you have handled challenging work situations in the past. The key is to demonstrate that you have learned from these challenging situations.

모든 면접 질문은 어려울 수 있지만 일부 유형의 질문은 더 어려울 수 있다. 면접관은 당신이 정답을 가지고 있는지 확인하기 위해 도전적인 면접 질문을 하는 것이 아니다. 그들은 도전적인 질문을 통해 당신이 어떻게 반응하는지 자신의 회사에 적합한지를 판단한다. 면접 질문 중 일부가 도전적이어도 당황하지 마라. 긍정적으로 생각하고 직책과 직업에 관한 기술과 경험의 구체적인 예를 포함한 논리적인 답변을 제공하라. 행동 면접 질문은 당신이 과거에 어려운 업무 상황에 어떻게 대처했는지와 관련이 있다. 중요한 것은 당신이 이러한 도전적인 상황에서 배웠다는 것을 증명하는 것이다.

Interview Questions
면접 질문

Q.1 How would you resolve conflicts in the workplace?
직장에서 갈등을 어떻게 해결할 것입니까?

Q.2 How would you handle an unsatisfied customer?
불만족을 느끼는 고객에게 어떻게 대처할 것입니까?

Q.3 Do you have any failure or disappointment in your life?
If so, what did you learn from the experience?

당신 인생에서 어떤 실패나 실망이 있었습니까?
그렇다면 그 경험을 통해 무엇을 배웠습니까?

Q.4 Describe a difficult work situation you have had and tell me how you handled it.

어려운 업무 상황에 대해 설명하고 대처하는 방법을 알려주십시오.

Q.5 How do you handle stress?

스트레스를 어떻게 해소하십니까?

Interview Questions & Sample Responses
면접 질문 및 응답 샘플

Q.1 How would you resolve conflicts in the workplace?

직장에서 갈등을 어떻게 해결할 것입니까?

R1 If I were having a conflict with a person in the workplace, I would want to talk with the person to identify the conflict. Then I would listen carefully to what he or she has to say and try to come up with a plan together that could resolve our conflict.

직장에 있는 사람과 갈등이 있는 경우 그 사람과 이야기 하여 갈등을 파악합니다. 그리고 상대방이 말한 것을 신중하게 경청하고 갈등을 함께 해결할 수 있는 계획을 세우려고 노력할 것입니다.

R2 If there is any problem in the workplace, I think it is important to carefully reflect about the problem before one can come up with a solution. Once the problem is understood, I would talk with the parties who are involved and discuss possible solutions.

직장에서 문제가 있는 경우 해결책을 제시하기 전에 문제에 대해 신중하게 생각하는 것이 중요하다고 생각합니다. 문제가 이해되면 당사자들과 이야기하고 가능한 해결책을 논의할 것입니다.

(R3) I believe one of the best ways to resolve conflicts in the workplace is to resolve it sooner than later. So if there is a conflict in the workplace, I would try to resolve it by meeting with the person whom I am having a problem to discuss the matter in a kindly manner. I would want to understand the situation from his/her perspective and try to figure out where the misunderstanding occurred.

직장에서 갈등을 해결하는 최선의 방법 중 하나는 늦기 전에 보다 빨리 해결하는 것이라고 생각합니다. 직장 내에서 갈등이 있는 경우, 문제가 있는 사람과 만나서 친절하게 문제를 상의하려고 노력할 것입니다. 저는 상대방의 관점에서 상황을 이해하고 오해가 어디에서 발생했는지 파악하려고 노력할 것입니다.

Your Response: 당신의 대답

Q.2 How would you handle an unsatisfied customer?

불만족을 느끼는 고객에게 어떻게 대처할 것입니까?

R1 If there were an unsatisfied customer, I would first try to find out why the customer is unsatisfied. After hearing the reason, I would first sincerely apologize for the incident that is bothering him/her. Then, I would find a solution that would comfort him/her.

불만족스러운 고객이 있다면 저는 먼저 고객이 만족하지 못하는 이유를 찾으려고 할 것입니다. 그 이유를 들은 후, 먼저 진심으로 그 고객을 불편하게 한것을 사과할 것입니다. 그런 다음 고객을 안심시킬 수 있는 해결책을 찾을 것입니다.

R2 I think it is important to understand the customer and the situation from the customer's perspective. I would listen attentively to the customer as he/she complains about the situation. Then, I would inform the customer that I would do my best to help him/her with the situation.

저는 고객의 관점에서 고객의 상황을 이해하는 것이 중요하다고 생각합니다. 고객이 상황에 대해 불평할 때 저는 주의 깊게 들을 것입니다. 그런 다음 고객의 상황을 돕기 위해 최선을 다할 것임을 안내할 것입니다.

R3 I would first listen attentively to the customer. Then, I would apologize for the situation. I think it is important to let the customer know that I understand his frustration. I would comfort the customer by saying that I would find a solution for him/her. If there is no solution to the problem, I would provide several options for the customer so he/she could select the best one for him.

저는 우선 고객의 의견을 주의깊게 경청할 것입니다. 그리고 그 상황에 대해 사과할 것입니다. 저는 고객에게 그의 불만을 이해한다고 알리는 것이 중요하다고 생각합니다. 고객에게 해결책을 찾아드릴 것이라고 안내함으로써 고객을 안심시킬 것입니다. 문제에 대한 해결책이 없다면 고객을 위한 몇 가지 선택사항을 제공하여 가장 적합한 사항을 선택할 수 있게 하겠습니다.

Your Response: 당신의 대답

Q.3 Do you have any failure or disappointment in your life?
If so, what did you learn from the experience?

당신 인생에서 어떤 실패나 실망이 있습니까?
그렇다면 그 경험에서 무엇을 배웠습니까?

R1 In the beginning of my college days, I was not very motivated to do well in school. I was more interested in making friends and going out with them. As a result, my grades suffered when I was a freshman in college. However, after realizing the consequences of my actions, I have turned my life around and began focusing on my studies. For my last year in college, I have received an academic scholarship because of my effort. I learned a lot from this experience.

대학 초반에, 저는 학교에서 잘 하고 싶은 동기가 별로 없었습니다. 저는 친구를 사귀고 그들과 함께 외출하는데 더 관심이 많았습니다. 그 결과, 저는 대학 1학년 때 좋지 않은 학업성적을 받게 되었습니다. 하지만, 제 행동의 결과를 깨닫고 제 주변

의 삶을 바꾸고 학업에 집중하기 시작했습니다. 그래서 저는 대학 마지막 해에 제 노력으로 성적 장학금을 받았습니다. 이 경험을 통해서 많은 것을 배웠습니다.

R2 I was disappointed after my first real job interview after college. I knew I failed in that interview because I did not prepare myself for the interview. After that experience, I have worked hard to better prepare myself for job interviews. I realized the best remedy after any failure is to learn from it.

대학 졸업 후 첫 취업 면접을 본 후 실망했습니다. 저는 면접 준비를 하지 않았기 때문에 그 면접에서 실패했음을 알았습니다. 그 경험 후, 저는 취업 면접을 준비하기 위해 열심히 노력했습니다. 어떤 실패 후 가장 좋은 해결책은 그것으로 부터 배우는 것임을 깨달았습니다.

R3 I don't usually have big disappointment in my life. I think because I am generally a positive person that even if I face any disappointment, I always try to think positively about it. I feel that there is always a lesson to learn from any disappointment or failure.

저는 보통 제 인생에서 큰 실망을 느끼지 않습니다. 저는 대체로 긍정적인 사람이기 때문에 어떤 실망에 직면하더라도 항상 긍정적으로 생각하려고 노력합니다. 저는 어떤 실망이나 실패로 부터 배울 수 있는 교훈이 항상 있다고 느낍니다.

Your Response: 당신의 대답

Q.4 Describe a difficult work situation you have had and tell me how you handled it.

어려운 업무 상황에 대해 설명하고 대처하는 방법을 알려주십시오.

R1 I did not have any difficulty while working. Once in a while, we had an employee who would call in sick at the last minute. So when that happened, it was difficult to meet the needs of customers because we were short-staffed. However, I always provided a smile and worked extra harder while serving customers.

직장에서 일 할 때 딱히 큰 어려움은 없었습니다. 가끔, 일을 시작하기 바로 직전에 아프다고 전화를 하는 직원이 있었습니다. 그때 우리는 직원이 부족해 고객의 요구를 충족시키기 어려웠습니다. 하지만 미소를 잃지 않고 없는 직원 몫까지 열심히 일했습니다.

R2 Sometimes we had difficulty meeting the needs of customers due to unexpected situations. For example, when we are out of stock with merchandise, we often order items for customers. But occasionally, few of the items would arrive with fault in them. When that happens, I always order the items again as soon as possible for customers.

가끔씩 예상치 못한 상황에서 고객들의 요구를 충족시키는 데에 어려움이 있었습니다. 예를 들어, 상품 재고가 없을 때 고객들을 위해 주문을 하곤 합니다. 하지만 경우에 따라, 몇몇 품목이 잘못 도착하는 경우가 있습니다. 그런 일이 발생하면 항상 고객을 위해 가능한 빨리 상품을 다시 주문합니다.

R3 I sometimes faced unfriendly and demanding customers. At first, I didn't know how to treat them. However, as time passed by, I became more confident serving them and satisfying their needs.

가끔은 불친절하고 요구가 많은 고객들을 응대 했습니다. 처음에는 어떻게 그들을 대해야 할지 몰랐습니다. 그러나 시간이 지나면서 그들을 위해 서비스를 제공하고 그들의 요구를 충족시키는데 자신감을 갖게 되었습니다.

Your Response: 당신의 대답

_____

_____

_____

_____

Key words and expressions • 핵심 단어와 표현

When difficult questions are asked, use the following expressions.

어려운 질문이 나올 때 다음과 같은 표현을 사용하라.

Could you give me a second to answer your question?

질문에 대답 할 수 있는 시간을 좀 주시겠습니까?

Well, let me think. Would you give me a second to think about the answer?

글쎄요, 생각 좀 해보겠습니다. 대답에 대해 잠시 생각할 시간을 주시겠습니까?

Well, that is a difficult question. I don't have any personal experience that could relate to the question, but I will do my best answering it.

글쎄요, 그것은 어려운 질문입니다. 저는 그 질문과 관련된 개인적인 경험은 없지만, 최선을 다해 대답해 보겠습니다.

Q.5 How do you handle stress?
스트레스를 어떻게 해소하십니까?

R1 I try not to get stressed because I know it is not healthy. However, if I do get stressed, I usually talk about what is bothering me with my close family or friends. I always feel much better after because I can see the problem from a different perspective.

스트레스가 건강에 좋지 않다는 것을 알고 있기 때문에 스트레스를 받지 않으려고 노력합니다. 그러나 스트레스를 받을 경우 가까운 가족이나 친구에게 저를 힘들게 하는 것에 대해 이야기 합니다. 다른 관점에서 문제를 볼 수 있기 때문에 이후에는 언제나 훨씬 더 기분이 좋아집니다.

R2 I usually exercise. And, ever since I started exercising I do not get stressed very much. If there is a problem I need to solve, I usually seek advice from the people who could help me.

저는 평소에 스트레스를 해결하기 위해 운동을 합니다. 그리고 운동을 시작한 이후로 별로 스트레스를 받지 않습니다. 해결해야 할 문제가 있다면, 보통 저를 도울 수 있는 사람들에게 조언을 구합니다.

R1 I consider myself positive and easy-going, so I am not the type of a person who stresses over things. But if I do get stressed, I would probably do things I enjoy doing, such as exercising or reading.

저는 제 자신을 긍정적이고 낙천적인 사람이라고 생각하기 때문에 특별히 스트레스를 받는 사람의 유형은 아닙니다. 그러나 스트레스를 받으면 운동이나 독서와 같이 제가 즐기는 일을 할 것입니다.

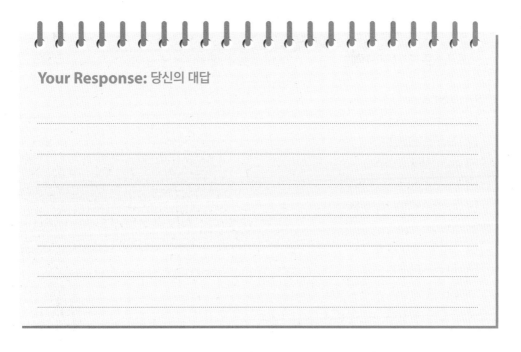

Your Response: 당신의 대답

Key words and expressions • 핵심 단어와 표현

1) To handle stress, ⋯

스트레스를 해소하기 위해⋯ 나는 _____ (무엇을) 한다.

- ☑ I usually take a break.
- ☑ I read books.
- ☑ I play the piano.
- ☑ I exercise.
- ☑ I listen to music.
- ☑ I watch a movie.
- ☑ I do yoga.
- ☑ I go for a drive.
- ☑ I eat delicious food.

2) I get rid of stress by…

스트레스를 해소하기 위해 _____을 한다.

- ☑ exercising.
- ☑ listening to music.
- ☑ taking a break.
- ☑ going for a drive.
- ☑ eating delicious food.
- ☑ meeting my friends.
- ☑ doing yoga.
- ☑ going camping.
- ☑ riding a bike.

 Let's Practice English • 영어를 연습해 보자

Activity 1: Writing/Speaking 쓰기/말하기

Please answer the following questions. Share your answer with your partner.
Then ask your partner some of his/her ways of managing stress.
다음 질문에 답하라. 답변을 파트너에게 공유하라. 그런 다음 파트너에게 스트레스 대처 방법에 대해 질문하라.

1) Did you encounter any difficulty while working?
   일을 하면서 어려움에 직면한 적은 없었습니까?

....

....

....

....

2) How do you handle stress?
스트레스를 어떻게 해소하십니까?

3) How do you maintain good health?
어떻게 건강을 유지합니까?

Success in English Interview for Cabin Crew: How to Win the Job Interview

항공 승무원을 위한 성공 영어 인터뷰:
면접에서 승리하는 방법

Chapter 08

Scenario/Role-Play Questions
시나리오/실제 상황극
면접 질문

Chapter 08

Scenario/Role-Play Questions
시나리오/실제 상황극 면접 질문

Chapter Goals 챕터 목표

- To identify scenario/role-play questions
  시나리오/실제 상황극 질문을 인식하기

- To use appropriate expressions to respond to scenario/role-play interview questions
  적절한 표현을 사용하여 시나리오/실제 상황극 면접 질문에 응답하기

Grammar Points 핵심 문법

Type 1 Conditional: Possible Results 직설법

The type 1 conditional sentences demonstrate situations that are possible in the present or future.

제 1 유형의 직설법 문장은 현재 또는 미래에 가능한 상황을 보여준다.

Condition 조건	Result 결과
If + subject + present simple	subject + helping verb + present simple
If 주어 + 동사 현재형	주어+ 조동사 현재형 + 동사 원형
If you get the next question correct,	you will win the game.
당신이 다음 질문을 맞추면,	이 게임에서 이길 겁니다.
If you make it to the next interview,	you will get the job.
다음 면접에 올라간다면,	당신은 이 직업을 얻을 것입니다.

Type 2 Conditional: Hypothetical Situations 가정법

The type 2 conditional sentences are not based on fact. The type 2 conditional sentences show situations that are hypothetical and provide probable results.

제 2 유형의 가정법 문장은 사실에 근거하지 않는다. 여기에서 쓰는 문장은 가설적인 상황을 보여 주며 가능한 결과를 제공한다.

Condition 조건 과거	Result 결과
If + subject + simple past	present conditional
If + 주어 + 과거 동사	주어+ 조동사 과거형 + 동사 원형
If you came late,	you would miss the party.
당신이 늦게 온다면,	파티를 놓칠 것입니다.
If you liked coffee,	I would buy you a coffee maker.
당신이 커피를 좋아한다면,	커피 메이커를 사 줄 것입니다.

Key Vocabulary 주요 어휘

refuse	remind	consequence
monitor	demand	surrounding

attentive	option	intoxicated
rude	mishap	proactive
fine	allow	instead
complimentary	laundry	incident

 ## Key Expressions 핵심 표현

See each section for key expressions.

각 부분에서 핵심 표현을 참조하라.

Interview Tips 면접 팁 •

Well-prepared candidates have go-to responses for common interview questions. However, for scenario or role-play questions, candidates need to think on their feet and provide well-thought-out responses. Employers ask scenario questions to discern candidates' ability to solve problems, but to also bring out their inner values related to the role of the job they are required to do if they are hired. When responding to the scenario or role-play questions, understand the situations and provide responses that are most appropriate for the situations.

잘 준비된 응시자는 일반적인 면접 질문에 대한 답변이 있다. 그러나 시나리오나 실제 상황극 면접 질문의 경우, 응시자는 자신의 생각을 잘 생각하고 답을 제공해야 한다. 고용주는 응시자의 문제 해결 능력을 구별하기 위해 시나리오 질문을 하고 또 그들이 고용됐을 경우 수행하는데 필요한 직업의 역할과 관련된 내면의 가치를 이해하는 면접 질문을 한다. 시나리오 또는 실제 상황극 면접 질문에 응답 할 때 상황을 잘 이해하고 상황에 가장 적합한 답을 제공하라.

Interview Questions
면접 질문

Q.1 How would you deal with a passenger who refuses to fasten the seatbelt?

안전벨트 착용을 거부하는 승객을 어떻게 대응하겠습니까?

Q.2 How would you deal with a drunken passenger who keeps asking for more alcohol?

만취한 승객이 계속해서 알코올을 원한다면 당신은 어떻게 대응하겠습니까?

Q.3 How would you deal with a demanding and rude passenger?

당신은 까다롭고 무례한 승객을 어떻게 대응하겠습니까?

Q.4 What would you do if there was a passenger smoking in the lavatory?

만약 승객이 화장실에서 흡연을 한다면 어떻게 하겠습니까?

Q.5 What would you do if you spilled juice or water to a passenger due to a sudden turbulence?

만약 갑작스러운 기류 변화로 인해 주스나 물을 승객에게 엎질렀다면 어떻게 하겠습니까?

Interview Questions & Sample Responses
면접 질문 및 응답 샘플

Q.1 How would you deal with a passenger who refuses to fasten the seatbelt?

안전벨트 착용을 거부하는 승객을 어떻게 대응하겠습니까?

R1 I would first ask the passenger if I could help him/her fasten the seatbelt. If the passenger refused, I would be very polite to let him/her know that all passengers are required to fasten their seatbelt when the seatbelt sign is on for safety reasons. If for any reason, the passenger still refused to fasten the seatbelt during landing or take-off, I would tell him/her that I would be reporting this matter to the security personnel and there could be consequences for his/her action.

저는 승객에게 안전벨트 착용을 도와줘도 되는지 먼저 물어볼 것입니다. 만약에 승객이 안전벨트 착용을 거절하는 경우, 안전벨트 표시가 켜졌을 때에는 안전상의 이유로 모든 승객이 안전벨트를 착용해야 한다는 사실을 정중하게 알릴 것입니다.

어떤 이유로 승객이 계속해서 착륙 또는 이륙 중 안전벨트 착용을 거부하는 경우, 이 문제를 보안 요원에게 보고 할 수밖에 없다고 말하고, 그/그녀의 행동에 대한 조치가 있을 것이라고 전하겠습니다.

R2 I would kindly remind the passenger that the captain has turned on the seatbelt sign on. So I would inform the passenger that everyone needs to fasten the seatbelt while the sign is on.

저는 친절하게 기장이 안전벨트 착용 사인을 켰음을 승객에게 상기시킵니다. 그래서 승객에게 안전벨트 착용 표시가 켜졌을 때에는 모든 승객이 안전을 위해 안전벨트를 착용해야 한다고 안내할 것입니다.

Your Response: 당신의 대답

Q.2 How would you deal with a drunken passenger who keeps asking for more alcohol?

만취한 승객이 계속해서 알코올을 원한다면 당신은 어떻게 대응하겠습니까?

R1 I would politely inform the passenger that he/she has had too much alcohol already. I would also politely inform the passenger for safety reasons, we are not allowed to serve alcohol to intoxicated passengers. I would kindly offer other beverages instead. If the passenger still continued to ask for more alcohol, I would let other crew members know of the situation to avoid serving more alcohol to the passenger.

저는 정중히 승객에게 이미 만취했음을 알릴 것입니다. 또한 안전상의 이유로 만취한 승객에게 알코올을 제공 할 수 없다고 공손하게 전할 것입니다. 대신 다른 음료를 친절하게 제공 할 것입니다. 승객이 계속 더 많은 알코올을 요구하는 경우, 추가 알코올을 제공하는 것을 피하기 위해 다른 승무원에게 상황을 전하겠습니다.

R2 For me, it is important to be proactive during boarding, so I would always check to ensure that no drunken passenger boards on the plane. I would also do my best to monitor passengers for their alcohol intake during in-flight. However, after taking these measures and I find a drunken passenger who keeps asking for more alcohol, I would politely inform the passenger that he/she has had too much alcohol. For public safety reasons I would firmly tell the passenger that I would not be able to serve any more alcohol. I would also inform my other team members, so they do not serve any more alcohol.

저에게는 승객들이 탑승하는 동안 사전 대책을 세우는 것이 중요합니다. 그래서 항상 비행기에 만취한 승객이 탑승하는지 확인합니다. 기내에서 알코올 섭취량을 모니터하기 위해 최선을 다할 것입니다. 그러나 이러한 조치를 취한 후 만취한 승객이 계속해서 더 많은 알코올을 요구한다면 저는 승객에게 알코올을 이미 많이 드셨음을 정중하게 알릴 것입니다. 안전상의 이유로 더 이상 알코올을 제공 할 수 없다는 사실을 승객에게 분명히 말합니다. 또한 더 이상 알코올을 제공 못하도록 다른 팀원들에게 알릴 것입니다.

Your Response: 당신의 대답

Q.3 How would you deal with a demanding and rude passenger?
당신은 까다롭고 무례한 승객을 어떻게 대응하겠습니까?

R1 Regardless of any situation, it is important for me to be professional and to be polite to all passengers. I would kindly listen to what the passenger is asking and find out if it is something I can help him/her. If the need is something I can assist with, I will gladly provide the assistance. If the passenger requested a demand that is out of my control, I would first sincerely apologize that the request cannot be completed and provide a good reason for it. I would then kindly provide other options to soothe the passenger.

어느 상황에 관계없이, 모든 승객에게 예의를 갖추며 전문적으로 행동하는 것이 중요합니다. 친절하게 승객이 요구하는 요청을 듣고 제가 승객을 도울 수 있는 일인지 확인 할 것입니다. 제가 도울 수 있는 요청이라면 기꺼이 도움을 제공 할 것입니다. 승객이 제 통제 범위를 벗어난 요구를 요청하는 경우, 요구사항을 수용할 수 없다는 점에 진심으로 사과드리고 타당한 이유를 설명할 것입니다. 그런 다음 승객을 가라앉힐 수 있는 다른 대안을 친절하게 제공할 것입니다.

R2 I would be attentive to the passenger's request and assist him/her with the request as politely as possible. If I am not able to assist the passenger with the request, I will provide another option. I would remain professional and not take the passenger's rudeness personally.

저는 승객의 요청에 주의를 기울이고 최대한 정중히 요청을 도와 줄 것입니다. 승객의 요청을 지원할 수 없는 경우 다른 대안을 제공할 것입니다. 저는 직업적인 정신을 유지하고 승객의 무례함을 개인적으로 받아들이지 않을 것입니다.

Your Response: 당신의 대답

🖥 Interview Tips 면접 팁 ● ● ● ● ● ● ● ● ● ● ● ● ● ●

The key is to first understand the situation, second apologize for the inconvenience, third provide an appropriate solution, and then provide a rationale for your solution. It is always a good idea to follow up with the passenger to check his/her condition.

중요한 것은 먼저 상황을 이해하고, 두 번째는 불편을 끼친 것을 사과하며, 세 번째는 적절한 해결책을 제공한 다음 해결책에 대한 근거를 제공하는 것이다. 승객의 상태를 확인하기 위해 승객을 후속 조치하는 것은 언제나 좋은 생각이다.

Understand the situation → Apologize for the inconvenience → Provide a solution → Provide a rationale for your solution → Follow-up to check on the situation

상황 파악/공감 → 불편에 대해 사과 → 해결책 제공 → 해결책에 대한 이유 설명 → 상황을 점검하고 후속 조치

Key words and expressions • 핵심 단어와 표현

To apologize 사과할 때

- ☑ I am sorry about the situation.
- ☑ I am very sorry for your inconvenience.
- ☑ Please accept our sincere apologies for this situation.
- ☑ I sincerely apologize for this.
- ☑ I am incredibly sorry for this situation.

To show empathy (understanding) 공감을 표시할 때

- ☑ I can understand how you feel.
- ☑ I understand your situation.
- ☑ I completely understand how you feel.
- ☑ Sure, I can see how you feel.
- ☑ I know you are upset and I understand how you feel.

To provide a solution/option 해결책/대안을 제공할때

☑ Could I offer you _____ instead?
☑ May I offer you _____ instead?
☑ How about if I offer you _____ ? Would that work for you?
☑ Could I provide you with _____ instead?

To provide a rationale (explanation) 이유를 설명할 때

☑ Because of our policy, we are not able to ……
☑ For safety reasons, all passenger are required to fasten their seatbelt when the seatbelt sign is on.
☑ Smoking in the plane is strictly prohibited.

(Q.4) **What would you do if there was a passenger smoking in the lavatory?**

만약 승객이 화장실에서 흡연을 한다면 어떻게 하겠습니까?

(R1) If I found out there was a passenger smoking in the lavatory, I would firmly ask the passenger to immediately put out the cigarette and to come out of the lavatory. I would first check the lavatory to ensure the cigarette is disposed of safely and properly. Then I would firmly inform the passenger that smoking on the plane is strictly prohibited. I would report this incident to the in-flight service manager.

만약에 승객이 화장실에서 흡연한 사실을 알게 된다면, 승객에게 즉시 담배를 끄고 화장실에서 나올 것을 단호하게 요구할 것입니다. 저는 먼저 담배가 안전하고 적절하게 처리되어 있는지 화장실을 점검 할 것입니다. 그리고 기내에서의 흡연은 엄격히 금지되어 있음을 승객에게 확실히 알릴 것입니다. 이 사건을 기내 서비스 관리자에게 보고 할 것입니다.

R2 I would strongly tell the passenger that he/she must immediately put out the cigarette and come out of the lavatory. After the passenger comes out, I would check the lavatory and the surrounding area for any smoke or fire. I would firmly inform the passenger that in-flight smoking is against the aviation regulations and there is a fine for violators. I would report this incident to the senior purser.

저는 승객에게 즉시 담배를 끄고 화장실에서 나와야한다고 강력히 말할 것입니다. 승객이 나온 후에는 화장실과 주변에 연기나 화재가 없는지 확인합니다. 기내에서의 흡연은 항공 규정에 위배되며 위반자에게 벌금이 부과된다는 사실을 승객에게 확실하게 알릴 것입니다. 저는 이 사건을 사무장에게 보고할 것입니다.

Your Response: 당신의 대답

Q.5 What would you do if you spilled juice or water to a passenger due to a sudden turbulence?

만약 갑작스러운 기류 변화로 인해 주스나 물을 승객에게 엎질렀다면 어떻게 하겠습니까?

R1 I would sincerely apologize for my mishap and help the passenger wipe the spill right away with a clean towel. If necessary, I would also offer a complimentary laundry coupon the passenger can use upon his/her arrival. I would apologize again and continue to check to make sure the passenger has a pleasant flight.

저의 실수에 대해 진심으로 사과할 것이고 승객이 깨끗한 수건으로 얼룩을 즉시 닦을 수 있도록 도와줄 것입니다. 필요한 경우 착륙 후 사용할 수 있는 무료세탁 쿠폰도 제공할 것입니다. 다시 사과하고 승객이 즐거운 비행이 되도록 계속 확인하겠습니다.

R2 I would sincerely apologize and apologize again. Then I would provide the passenger with a clean towel and help him/her wipe the spill. I would inform the passenger that there is a complimentary laundry coupon he/she can use after landing.

진심으로 사과하고 또 사과할 것입니다. 그런 다음 승객에게 깨끗한 수건을 제공하고 얼룩을 닦을 수 있도록 도와줍니다. 착륙 후 사용할 수 있는 무료 세탁 쿠폰이 있음을 승객에게 알려드릴 것입니다.

Your Response: 당신의 대답

Let's Practice English • 영어를 연습해 보자

Activity 1: Speaking/Listening 말하기/듣기

Please read the following questions and understand the situations. Respond to the questions with appropriate responses. Then ask your partner with the questions and find out what he/she would do in those situations?

다음 질문을 읽고 상황을 이해하라. 적절한 응답으로 질문에 답변하라. 그런 다음 파트너에게 질문을 하고 그 상황에서 그/그녀가 어떻게 답변 할 것인지를 알아보아라.

Q: What would you do if ... ?

R: I would ...

1) What would you do if you needed to learn another foreign language in a very short time?

My response:

My partner's response:

2) What would you do if you accidentally forgot your best friend's birthday?

My response:

My partner's response:

3) What would you do if your classmate kept asking to use your cell phone?

My response:

My partner's response:

4) What would you do if you forgot to bring your homework?

My response:

My partner's response:

5) What would you do if your classmate always borrowed money from you?

My response:

My partner's response:

Success in English Interview for Cabin Crew:
How to Win the Job Interview

항공 승무원을 위한 성공 영어 인터뷰:
면접에서 승리하는 방법

Chapter 09

Researching Employers
고용주 조사하기

Chapter 09

Researching Employers
고용주 조사하기

 Chapter Goals 챕터 목표

✡ To understand the importance of researching employers
고용주를 조사하는 중요성 이해하기

✡ To identify common interview questions about employers
고용주에 관한 일반적인 면접 질문 확인하기

✡ To use appropriate expressions to respond to interview questions about employers
적절한 표현을 사용하여 고용주에 관한 면접 질문에 응답하기

 Grammar Points 핵심 문법

The Superlative: Comparing Three or More Items
최상급: 셋 이상의 비교

When we compare three or more items in a group, we use the superlative form of the adjective.
그룹에서 셋 이상의 사람과 또는 물건을 비교할 때 최상급 형용사를 사용한다.

One-syllable adjectives: add the --est

The _____ airline is the safest airline in the skies.

Two-syllable adjectives ending in --y: change y to i and add the --est

The _____ airline is the friendliest airline of all airlines.

Adjectives with two or more syllables: use the most or the least

The _____ airline is the most comfortable airline in the world.

The _____ airline is the least expensive airline in Korea.

Key Vocabulary 주요 어휘

reputable	mannerism	ultimate
launch	competitive	destination
initially	established	promptly
possess	carrier	impressed
exceptional	interact	sophisticated

Key Expressions 핵심 표현

See each section for key expressions.

각 부분에서 핵심 표현을 참조하라.

🖼 Interview Tips 면접 팁 •

When applying for jobs, one of the most important processes is to do research on employers. However, many job applicants often neglect the process and do not see the importance of it. When you make the time to do research, it helps you identify the right places to apply that match your interests and qualifications. You can also make a good impression on the application during the interview when you know a lot about the company because it makes you stand out among other candidates.

입사를 지원할 때, 가장 중요한 과정 중 하나는 고용주에 대해 조사를 하는 것이다. 그러나 많은 구직자들은 종종 그 과정을 무시하고 그것의 중요성을 알지 못한다. 조사할 시간을 갖는다면 관심분야 및 자격요건에 맞는 적절한 직업을 파악하는데 도움이 된다. 또한 회사에 대해 많은 것을 알고 있을 때 다른 응시자들 중에서도 눈에 띄는 응시자로 만들기 때문에 지원서 및 면접에서 좋은 인상을 줄 수 있다.

Doing research can 조사를 통해

help you identify the most suitable companies that meet your interest and qualifications.

당신의 관심과 자격을 충족시키는 가장 적합한 회사를 찾는데 도움이 된다.

demonstrate your enthusiasm and interest in the company.

회사에 대한 열정과 관심을 보여준다.

help you tailor your resume and cover letter to emphasize your pertinent skills and experiences that match the needs of your employer.

이력서와 커버 레터를 맞춤화하여 고용주의 요구에 부합하는 적절한 기술과 경험을 강조한다.

help you prepare for questions to ask during an interview.

면접에서 물어볼 질문을 준비하는데 도움을 준다.

help you stand out among other candidates.

당신이 다른 응시자들 중에서 눈에 띄도록 도와준다.

help you be more prepared.
당신이 더 준비되도록 도와준다.

👥 Interview Questions
면접 질문

Q.1 Why do you want to work for this airline (company)?
왜 이 항공사 (회사)에서 일하기 원하십니까?

Q.2 Who are the major competitors of this airline (company)?
이 항공사 (회사)의 주요 경쟁자는 누구입니까?

Q.3 What do you know about our airline (company)?
우리 항공사 (회사)에 대해 무엇을 아십니까?

Q.4 How has your education/experience prepared you for your career?
당신의 경력을 위해 교육/경험을 어떻게 준비해 왔습니까?

Q.5 What can you contribute to this company?
이 회사에 당신은 무엇을 기여하겠습니까?

🔤 Interview Questions & Sample Responses
면접 질문 및 응답 샘플

Q.1 Why do you want to work for this airline (company)?
왜 이 항공사 (회사)에서 일하기를 원하십니까?

R1 I have always admired your company because it is one of the most reputable companies in Korea. Your company has a very strong reputation and a positive image with its customers. In recent years, your company has even earned international awards for providing excellent service to its customers. I would like to use the service skills I gained from my educational and work experience to make a positive contribution to your company.

저는 귀사가 한국에서 가장 평판이 좋은 회사 중 하나이기 때문에 항상 귀하의 회사에 감탄했습니다. 귀사는 고객들로 부터 매우 강력한 평판과 긍정적인 이미지를 가지고 있습니다. 최근 몇 년 동안 귀사는 고객에게 우수한 서비스를 제공한 것으로 인해 국제적인 상을 수상했습니다. 저의 교육 및 업무 경험에서 얻은 서비스 기술을 사용하여 귀사에 긍정적인 기여를 하고 싶습니다.

R2 My family and I have been using your airline ever since I was very young. We chose your airline whenever we traveled because of our positive experience. I was not only impressed with the service provided by the crew members but also with their professional mannerism. It is my dream to become a flight attendant, but to work for an airline that is the best in the business will be my ultimate dream.

제가 어렸을 때부터 저희 가족과 저는 계속 귀하의 항공사를 이용하고 있었습니다. 긍정적인 경험으로 인해 우리는 여행을 할 때마다 귀하의 항공사를 선택했습니다. 저는 승무원들에 의해 제공된 서비스 뿐만 아니라 그들의 전문적인 태도에 깊은 인상을 받았습니다. 승무원이 되는 것이 저의 꿈이지만, 항공업계에서 가장 좋은 항공사에서 일하는 것은 제 최고의 꿈입니다.

R3 It is important for me to work for a company that values commitment, community work, and diversity. Your company is known to have a long history of doing good work in the community and valuing diversity. It would be my honor to work for a company with such qualities.

저에게는 헌신, 지역사회 활동 및 다양성을 중시하는 회사에서 일하는 것이 중요합니다. 귀하의 회사는 지역사회에서 좋은 일을 하고 다양성을 존중하는 오랜 역사를 가진 것으로 알려져 있습니다. 그러한 자질을 갖춘 회사에서 일한다는 것이 저에겐 영광입니다.

Your Response: 당신의 대답

📷 Interview Tips 면접 팁 •

Interviewers ask this question to find out if you know their company and the competition. Do research on your company and find out who the competitors are. It would be helpful if you can share some facts and numbers. Perhaps the information you find is not as great as the competitors. But the key is to leave on a positive note.

면접관은 이 질문을 통해 자신이 속한 회사와 경쟁자를 알고 있는지 확인한다. 기업에 대한 조사를 수행하고 경쟁업체가 누구인지 알아보라. 몇 가지 사실과 통계를 공유할 수 있다면 도움이 될 것이다. 아마 당신이 찾은 정보는 경쟁자의 정보만큼 위대하지 않을 수도 있다. 그러나 중요한 것은 긍정적인 정보를 남기는 것이다.

Q.2 Who are the major competitors of this airline (company)?

이 항공사 (회사)의 주요 경쟁자는 누구입니까?

R1 The top Korean competitor for your airline is _____.
However, your airline still remains number one in Korea.

The top two foreign airlines that are considered as the major competitors of your airline are _____ and _____.

귀하의 항공사에서 최상위의 한국 경쟁자는 _____ 입니다. 그러나 귀하의 항공사는 여전히 한국에서 1위를 유지하고 있습니다. 항공사의 주요 경쟁자로 간주되는 상위 2개 외국항공사는 _____ 와 _____ 입니다.

R2 The top three competitors of your company are _____, _____ , and _____. Last year _____ company was number one in sales, but your company gained more market share.

귀사의 상위 3개의 경쟁 업체는 _____, _____, _____ 입니다. 작년 _____ 회사는 매출 1위를 차지했지만 귀사는 더 많은 시장 점유율을 확보했습니다.

R3 Your major competitor of your airline is _____. Although your airline carried out a similar number of destinations to your major competitor, last year your airline launched three new flight routes in _____. This is great news for customers and for the company as it can increase the market share and competitiveness.

귀사의 주요 경쟁자는 _____ 입니다. 귀사의 항공사는 주요 경쟁 업체와 비슷한 수의 목적지를 운영하고 있지만, 귀사는 작년에 세 개의 새로운 항공편 노선을 _____ 에 출시했습니다. 이는 시장 점유율과 경쟁력을 향상시킬 수 있어 고객과 회사 모두에게 좋은 소식입니다.

Your Response: 당신의 대답

Q.3 **What do you know about our airline (company)?**

우리 항공사 (회사)에 대해 무엇을 압니까?

R1 I know that your airline was initially established as the national airline in _____, but it became a private airline in _____. Now your airline is considered as the largest airline in _____ and has the most international and domestic flights and destinations. Your airline serves in _____ cities in _____ countries. For domestic division, it serves _____ destinations. Last year your airline created two new routes in _____. There are around _____ employees working for your airline.

귀하의 항공사가 처음에는 _____의 국영 항공사로 설립되었지만 _____의 민간 항공사가 되었음을 알고 있습니다. 지금은 귀 항공사는 _____에서 가장 큰 항공사로 간주되며 가장 많은 국제선 및 국내선 행선지가 있습니다. 귀하의 항공사는 _____ 국가의 _____ 도시에서 서비스 합니다. 국내 노선의 경우 행선지를 제공 한다고 알고 있습니다. 작년에 귀 항공사는 _____에서 두개의 새로운 경로를 만들었습니다. 귀 항공사에서 일하는 직원이 약 _____ 있다고 들었습니다.

R2 As of __(year)__, your airline is ranked _____ amongst the top _____ air carriers worldwide in terms of international passengers carried. Your airline includes many other subsidiary airlines, such as _____, _____, and _____. In __(year)__, your airline received a _____ award for its excellent service provided to passengers.

현재 _____ 년 기준으로, 귀하의 항공사는 국제선 탑승객의 관점에서 전 세계 일류 항공사 중 등급 _____ 위입니다. 귀하의 항공사에는 _____, _____, _____ 과 같은 많은 다른 보조 항공사가 포함되어 있습니다. _____ (해) _____ 년도에 귀하의 항공사는 승객에게 제공되는 탁월한 서비스로 _____ 상을 받았습니다.

R3 Your airline is a major airline in _____. It serves both domestic and international flights and destinations. Over _____ flights each day, it is considered as one of the oldest and biggest carriers in the _____ region. It was found in _____ and has over _____ joint partners.

귀하의 항공사는 _____에서 주요 항공사입니다. 국내선과 국제선 행선지를 모두 운행합니다. 매일 _____회 이상 운행되며 _____ 지역에서 가장 오래되고 큰 항공사 중 하나로 여겨집니다. 귀 항공사는 _____에 설립되었고 공동 파트너가 _____ 이상 있습니다.

Your Response: 당신의 대답

Interview Tips 면접 팁 •

Research the company you are interested in to find out what kind of product or service it provides and to whom. Understand the size of the company. Is it a large or a small company? How many people does the company employ? Be familiar with the company's history, achievements, goals, and values. Start with the company's website. If available, it is a good idea to also visit the company's Facebook, Twitter, and Google to find the most current information available. Also, talk to the people who are currently employed and/or who have previously worked in the industry.

관심 있는 회사를 조사하여 어떤 종류의 제품이나 서비스가 누구에게 제공되는지 확인하라. 회사의 규모를 이해하라. 큰 회사인가 작은 회사인가? 회사 직원은 몇 명인가? 회사의 연혁, 업적, 목표 및 가치에 대해 잘 알고 있어야 한다. 회사의 웹 사이트에서 시작하라. 가능한 경우 최신 정보를 찾으려면 회사의 Facebook, Twitter 및 Google을 방문하는 것이 좋다. 또한 현재 고용되어 있거나 이전에 업계에서 일했던 사람들과 이야기하라.

- ☑ What is the company's mission statement?
  회사의 사명 선언문은 무엇입니까?

- ☑ When was the company established?
  회사는 언제 설립 되었습니까?

- ☑ How big/small is the company?
  얼마나 큰/작은 회사입니까?

- ☑ Approximately how many people work for the company?
  얼마나 많은 사람들이 회사에서 일하고 있습니까?

- ☑ What is famously known for the company? (i.e., customer service, low fares, many routes, and etc.)
  회사에서 유명하게 알려진 것은 무엇입니까? (즉, 고객 서비스, 저렴한 요금, 많은 경로 등)

- ☑ What types of aircrafts and approximately how many aircrafts?
  어떤 종류의 항공기와 대략 얼마나 많은 항공기가 있습니까?

- ☑ Who is the company's major competitor?
  회사의 주요 경쟁자는 누구입니까?

- ☑ What is the latest news on the company?
  회사의 최신 뉴스는 무엇입니까?

Q.4 How has your education/experience prepared you for your career?

당신의 경력을 위해 교육/경험을 어떻게 준비해 왔습니까?

R1 I have customer service experience working at a department store and at a family restaurant for more than three years combined. Since I needed to work with many different types of customers everyday, I learned sophisticated service manners and effective communication skills in order to meet the needs of various customers. I believe my service experience will be useful when I work as a flight attendant.

저는 3년 이상 백화점과 패밀리 레스토랑에서 고객서비스 업무경험을 쌓았습니다. 매일 다른 유형의 고객을 만나며 일을 해야했기 때문에, 저는 수준 높은 서비스 매너와 효과적인 의사소통 능력으로 다양한 고객을 만족시켜야 했습니다. 저의 서비스 경험이 제가 승무원으로 일할 때 유용할 것이라고 믿습니다.

R2 I am currently working as a front desk receptionist at a hotel. Everyday I interact via telephone and in person with various hotel guests. Also, when customer issues arise, I have to solve them promptly and professionally. I believe my current experience will be very useful for this cabin crew position because I have gained excellent service skills.

저는 현재 호텔 프런트 데스크에서 일하고 있습니다. 매일 저는 다양한 호텔 고객들과 직접 또는 전화로 소통합니다. 또한 고객에게 문제가 발생하면, 신속하고 전문적으로 해결해야 합니다. 저는 훌륭한 서비스 기술을 습득했기 때문에 이러한 지금의 경험이 승무원이 되는 데에 매우 유용할 것이라고 믿습니다.

R3 I majored in airline service in college. For this major, I took relevant courses that are useful and valuable. Some of the courses include service manners, airline ticketing and reservations, flight announcement and various foreign language courses. I also have two years of working experience in the service industry.

저는 대학에서 항공서비스를 전공 했습니다. 이 전공 과정에서 유용하고 가치 있는 관련 강좌를 수강했습니다. 서비스 매너, 항공·발권과 예약, 기내 방송과 다양한 언어 수업을 포함한 강의들이 있었습니다. 저는 또한 2년의 서비스 분야 직무경험이 있습니다.

Your Response: 당신의 대답

Q.5 What can you contribute to this company?

이 회사에 당신은 무엇을 기여하겠습니까?

R1 I possess a combination of skills and experience that will be useful to work as a flight attendant. I have a degree in airline service and I have more than two years of experience working in the service industry. I will use my skills and experience to make positive contributions to your company.

저는 승무원으로 일하는데 유용한 기술과 경험을 보유하고 있습니다. 항공서비스 분야의 학위를 갖고 있으며 서비스 업계에서 2년 이상의 경력을 쌓았습니다. 제 능력과 경험을 이용하여 귀사에 긍정적인 기여를 하고 싶습니다.

R2 I consider myself a quick learner and self-motivated. Even though I was involved in many activities at my school, I still maintained excellent grades. I also have overseas experience that has helped me become a fluent English speaker. Because of my characteristics, I was able to achieve positive results in school and outside of school. I believe I can also obtain excellent results for your company.

저는 제 자신을 빠른 학습자이자 자발적인 사람이라고 생각합니다. 저는 학교에서 많은 활동에 참여했지만, 여전히 우수한 성적을 유지했습니다. 저는 또한 유창한 영어 실력을 갖추도록 도와준 해외 경험을 가지고 있습니다. 저의 특성 때문에 학교와 사회에서 긍정적인 결과를 얻을 수 있었습니다. 제가 귀사에서 일할 때 또한 우수한 결과를 얻을 수 있다고 믿습니다.

R3 I will be a great addition to your company because I am a committed and exceptional team player. My leadership activities at school can demonstrate my excellent teamwork skills. For example, I served as president of my school committee council and successfully led many different school festivals.

저는 헌신적이고 탁월한 팀 플레이어이기 때문에 귀사에 큰 도움이 될 것입니다. 학교에서의 리더십 활동을 통하여 훌륭한 팀워크 기술을 입증 할 수 있습니다. 예를 들어, 저는 학교위원회 대표를 역임하고 많은 다양한 학교 축제를 성공적으로 이끌었습니다.

Your Response: 당신의 대답

Let's Practice English • 영어를 연습해 보자

Activity 1: Writing 쓰기

Do research on three companies you would like to apply. Write down five interesting facts about the company.

신청하고 싶은 세 회사에 대해 조사를 하라. 회사에 관한 다섯 가지 흥미로운 사실을 적어보아라.

Use the following questions to do research:
조사를 위해 다음 질문을 사용하라:

☑ What is the company's mission statement?

  회사의 사명 선언문은 무엇입니까?

☑ When was the company established?

  회사는 언제 설립 되었습니까?

☑ How big/small is the company?

  얼마나 큰/작은 회사입니까?

☑ Approximately how many people work for the company?

  얼마나 많은 사람들이 회사에서 일하고 있습니까?

☑ What is famously known for the company? (i.e., customer service, low fares, many routes, and etc.)

  회사에서 유명하게 알려진 것은 무엇입니까? (즉, 고객 서비스, 저렴한 요금, 많은 경로 등)

☑ What types of aircrafts and approximately how many aircrafts?

  어떤 종류의 항공기와 대략 얼마나 많은 항공기가 있습니까?

☑ Who is the company's major competitor?

  회사의 주요 경쟁자는 누구입니까?

☑ What is the latest news on the company?

  회사의 최신 뉴스는 무엇입니까?

Company 1

Company 2

Company 3

Activity 2: Reading/Speaking 읽기/말하기

Take turns sharing the information you learned from activity 1 with your partner. 활동 1에서 배운 정보로 파트너와 공유하는 시간을 갖자.

- ☑ What did you learn from your partner's information?

  파트너의 정보를 통해 무엇을 배웠습니까?

- ☑ What information was interesting?

  어떤 정보가 흥미로웠습니까?

- ☑ What information was surprising for you and your partner?

  파트너로 부터 얻은 놀라운 정보는 무엇입니까?

- ☑ What information was useful for a job application?

  구직 신청에 유용한 정보는 무엇입니까?

Success in English Interview for Cabin Crew: How to Win the Job Interview

항공 승무원을 위한 성공 영어 인터뷰:
면접에서 승리하는 방법

Chapter 10

Resume & Cover Letter Writing Techniques

이력서 & 커버 레터 쓰기 기술

Chapter 10

Resume & Cover Letter Writing Techniques
이력서 & 커버 레터 쓰기 기술

Introduction
서론

Before anyone can be invited for a job interview, he or she must submit a job application with necessary and required documents to the company. Only if the company is satisfied with the candidate's application documents, the company will invite him/her for an interview. Thus, the first step to obtain a successful employment is to prepare strong job application documents. These necessary documents are a job application, a resume/curriculum vitae, and a cover letter. Most domestic airlines have their own job application requirements, so it is best to follow their guidelines and submit what is required for each airline. However, most foreign airlines and companies often require a resume/curriculum vitae and a cover letter with the job application.

누구든지 취업 면접에 초대되기 전에 필요한 문서 작업 신청서를 회사에 제출해야 한다. 회사가 직원 응시자의 신청서에 만족하는 경우에만 회사에서 인터뷰를 요청할 것이다. 따라서 성공적인 취업을 위한 첫 번째 단계는 뛰어난 직업 신청 서류를 준비하는 것이다. 이 필요한 서류는 취업 지원서, 이력서 (resume)/(curriculum vitae) 및 커버 레터 이다. 대부분의 국내 항공사는 자신의 취업 지원 요건을 가지고 있으므로 가이드라인을 준수하고 각 항공사에 필요한 것을 제출하는 것이 가장 좋다. 그러나 대부분의 외국 항공사와 회사는 이력서와 커버 레터 및 취업 지원서를 요구한다.

Curriculum Vitae vs. Resume: What is the difference?
커리큘럼 이력서 대 이력서 : 차이점은 무엇인가?

When applying for jobs, some prospective employers request a resume or a curriculum vitae (CV). Curriculum vitae is more commonly referred to as CV. While a resume or a curriculum vitae are both used for job applications, depending on the fields you are in, some employers prefer a resume or a CV. The main differences between a resume and a CV are the length and the information included in them. CVs are typically much longer than resumes. CVs include more detailed information of one's academic background, including awards, publications, presentations, other achievements as well as any work experience. Depending on one's experience and achievements, CVs can range from three to ten pages or longer. In America, CVs are used for positions in academia, research, education, and medicine. CVs are more often used in countries outside of the United States.

취업을 신청할 때 일부 예비 고용주는 이력서 또는 CV (이력서)를 요청한다. 일반적으로 curriculum vitae 이력서를 CV 라고 불린다. Resume 이력서 또는 커리큘럼 이력서는 직업 분야에 모두 사용되지만, 분야에 따라 일부 고용주는 Resume 이력서 또는 CV 이력서를 선호한다. Resume 이력서와 CV 이력서의 주요 차이점은 내용의 분량과 그 안에 포함된 정보 이다. CV는 일반적으로 Resume 이력서보다 훨씬 분량이 많다. CV 이력서에는 상, 출판물, 연구 발표, 기타 업적뿐만 아니라 모든 직업 경험을 포함하여 학업 배경에 대한 자세한 정보 가 포함 된다. 경험과 업적에 따라 CV는 3 – 10 페이지 이상이 될 수 있다. 미국에서 CV 이력 서는 학계, 연구, 교육 및 의학 분야의 직책에 사용되고 있다. CV는 미국 이외의 국가에서 더 많이 사용한다.

Resumes provide a brief summary of one's education, work experience, skills, and other accomplishments. Resumes also include an objective statement that tells the reader what type of position you are seeking. The information presented in the resume should inform the reviewer who you are, what your qualifications are, and any brief details of your working experiences. Based on the information, the prospective employer determines whether you should be invited for an interview. In most cases, the employer takes less than thirty seconds to review and to screen each incoming resume. Thus, your resume needs to be concise and clearly written with relevant work experiences and skills to inform the employer that you are qualified and suitable for the job. If your resume gets you an interview, your resume has done its job. Typically, a resume is only one page long and is concisely written in bullet points.

Resume 이력서는 교육, 업무 경험, 기술 및 기타 업적에 대한 간략한 요약을 제공한다. 이력서에는 당신이 희망하는 지원 분야 또는 찾는 부서의 직업 목표를 독자에게 알려주는 객관적인 진술이 포함된다. 이력서에 제시된 정보는 당신이 누구인지, 당신의 자격 요건 및 근무 경험에 대한 간략한 내용을 검토자에게 알려야한다. 이 정보를 바탕으로 예비 고용주는 당신이 면담을 위해 초대 받아야하는지 여부를 결정하는 것이다. 대부분의 경우, 고용주는 30 초 이내에 각 이력서를 검토하고 심사한다. 따라서 이력서는 당신이 자격을 갖추고 직업에 적합하다는 것을 고용주에게 알리기 위해 관련 업무 경험 및 기술을 통해 간결하고 명확하게 작성되어야한다. 당신의 이력서로 면접의 기회를 얻을 경우, 좋은 이력서를 만들었다는 증거이다. 일반적으로 이력서는 한 페이지에 불과하며 중요 항목으로 간결하게 작성되어있다.

Select Your Resume Type 이력서 유형 선택

When creating a resume, there are several different types of resumes to choose from. The most common formats are chronological, functional, and combination of the two. Depending on your situation, you can select to write a chronological, functional, or combination resume. Each resume type has its own uses and purposes.

이력서를 만들 때 선택할 수 있는 여러 가지 유형의 이력서가 있다. 가장 보편적인 형식은 (chronological resume) 연대순, (functional resume) 기능적인 것, 그리고 이 둘의 (combination resume) 조합이다. 상황에 따라 연대순, 기능적 또는 복합 이력서를 쓸 수 있다. 각 이력서 유형에는 자체 용도와 목적이 있다.

Chronological Resume 연대순 이력서

The chronological resume is more beneficial if you have solid and continuous work experience. Thus, if this is your first time applying for a job after graduation and/or you do not have any work experience, the chronological resume is not the appropriate one to use. This type of resume is useful for employers to see what jobs you have held and how long you have held those positions.

(Chronological Resume) 연대순 이력서는 지속적이고 탄탄한 업무 경험이 있는 경우 더 유용하다. 따라서 졸업 후 첫 번째 직업을 신청하는 경우 경험이 없다면 연대순 이력서는 적절한 것이 아니다. 이 유형의 이력서는 고용주가 당신이 어떤 직책을 맡았는지 여부와 그 직책을 얼마나 오랫동안 유지했는지 확인하는 데 유용하다.

Functional Resume 기능 이력서

A functional resume includes information about your skills and capabilities rather than information on your work experience. The functional resume is more advantageous to use if you are changing careers or if you are entering the job market for the first time. Since the functional resume does not focus on job experience, having an achievement section that outlines various skills that you have acquired throughout the years will be more useful rather than having a work experience section.

(Functional Resume) 기능 이력서는 직장 경험에 대한 정보가 아니라 기술 및 능력에 대한 정보가 포함되어 있다. 이 이력서는 직업을 바꾸거나 처음으로 취업에 입문하는 경우에 사용하는 것이 더 유리하다. 기능 이력서는 직업 경험에 초점을 두지 않으므로 실무 경험이 있는 섹션이 아닌 지난 몇 년 동안 습득한 다양한 기술을 요약한 업적 섹션이 있으면 더 유용한 정보가 된다.

Combination of Chronological and Functional Resume 조합 이력서

A combination resume highlights the important aspects of a chronological resume and a functional resume. Thus, the combination resume focuses on your skills and competencies as well as the context of where and when you have acquired these skills. The combination resume can help you emphasize on the skills that are relevant to the job you are applying for and provide information of the context where your skills were developed.

(Combination Resume) 조합 이력서는 연대순 이력서 및 기능 이력서의 중요한 측면을 강조 한다. 따라서 조합 이력서는 당신의 기술과 역량뿐만 아니라 당신이 이러한 기술을 취득한 시기와 상황에 초점을 맞추고 있다. 조합 이력서는 신청하는 직무와 관련된 기술을 강조하고 자신의 기술이 개발된 상황에 대한 정보를 제공하는 데 도움을 줄 수 있다.

Resume Writing Tips 이력서 쓰는 팁

When you see a good advertisement, what thought comes to your mind? If the advertisement was effective, you would want to purchase the product that the advertisement was advertising. A resume is similar to an advertisement. Think of yourself as the product to be advertised. What are the benefits of the product? The benefits can be thought of as your qualifications, skills, abilities, and/or accomplishments that can make positive influences to the company in which you are applying. In order to create an effective resume, you need to tailor your resume to the needs and specific jobs of your prospective employers. Do research on your prospective employers and find out what they are looking for. The more you know about your employers, you will understand their needs. Understanding your employers helps to create a resume that can make an impact.

좋은 광고를 볼 때 어떤 생각이 떠오르는가? 광고가 효과적이라면 광고한 제품을 구입하고 싶을 것이다. 이력서는 광고와 비슷하다. 자신을 광고 대상 제품으로 생각하면 좋다. 제품의 장점은 무엇인가? 혜택은 당신이 신청하는 회사에 긍정적 인 영향을 미칠 수 있는 당신의 자격, 기술, 능력 및 업적으로 간주 될 수 있다. 효과적인 이력서를 작성하려면 예비 고용주의 필요와 특정 직무에 맞게 이력서를 작성해야 한다. 예비 고용주에 대해 조사하고 그들이 찾고 있는 것을 알아라. 고용주에 대해 더 많이 알면 그들의 요구를 이해하게 될 것이다. 고용주를 이해하면 긍정적인 영향을 줄 수 있는 이력서를 작성하는 데 도움이 된다.

What to Include on Your Resume 이력서에 포함 할 내용

Personal Data/Information 개인 데이터 / 정보

Include your name, address, home phone number & cell number, and email address at the top of your resume in the personal information section. You can choose to include personal information at the top or on the left margin. Always use a professional email address. If you do not have a professional email address, create one.

이력서 상단에 당신의 이름, 주소, 집 전화 번호 및 휴대폰 번호, 이메일 주소를 개인 정보 섹션에 기재하라. 상단 또는 왼쪽 여백에 개인 정보를 포함하도록 선택할 수 있다. 항상 전문적인 이메일 주소를 사용하라. 전문 이메일 주소가 없다면 이메일 주소를 만들어라.

Career Objective 직업 목표

State the position you are seeking and focus on positive traits of your personality and skills that would make you a valuable employee.

희망하는 직업 목표나 해당부서를 적고, 가치 있는 직원이 될 만한 긍정적인 성격과 기술을 가지고 있다는 것에 초점을 맞춘다.

Work Experience/Employment History 직업 경력

List each job held and describe what you did in each job. Do not use personal pronouns. Start sentences with verbs that show action. Also, include dates and location (city and country) of your employment. Start with the most recent employment.

각 직업을 작성하고 그 직업에서 무엇을 했는지 설명하라. 개인 대명사(예를 들어, '나는') 주어를 사용하지 말고, 행동을 보여주는 동사로 문장을 시작하라. 또한 고용 날짜 및 지역(시 및 국가)을 포함하라. 가장 최근의 고용된 경력부터 시작하면 된다.

Education 학력

List the names of colleges and dates of degrees received with the most recent degree listed first. Also, include the locations and any honors received. Grade point average (GPA) can be included if yours is impressive.

가장 최근 학위가 수여된 학위명 및 날짜를 기재하라. 또한 학위를 받은 지역이나 국가를 기재하고, 대학에서 받은 상훈(표창)이 있다면 포함 시켜도 좋다. 자신의 점수가 인상적인 경우 평점 평균 (GPA)를 포함 할 수 있다.

Areas of Skills/Achievement 기술 분야 / 업적

List the skills/achievements you have developed and/or earned from your jobs or activities.

당신의 직업이나 활동으로 얻은 기술 / 업적을 기재한다.

Extracurricular/School Activities & Volunteer Work
동아리/자연봉사 활동

List each school/volunteer activity and describe what you did in each activity.

각 학교에서의 동아리활동과 자원봉사를 기재하고 각 활동에서 무엇을 했는지 요약한다.

What is a Cover Letter?
커버 레터 란 무엇인가?

커버레터(Cover Letter)란, 지원자가 희망하는 지원부서, 지원 분야 및 자신의 자격 등을 설명하는 개인 자기소개서가 포함된 편지글 형식의 표지 문서를 의미한다.

When you are applying for a job, a cover letter is accompanied by a resume. While a resume provides a brief summary of one's education, work experience, skills, and other accomplishments in bullet points, a cover letter is a written document that explains the applicant's interest in the position as well as his/her qualifications. Most companies read a cover letter before reviewing a resume.

취업을 신청할 때 이력서와 더불어 커버 레터 (Cover Letter) 라고 하는 자기소개를 첨부해야 한다. 이력서는 교육, 업무 경험, 기술 및 기타 업적에 대한 간략한 요약을 제공하지만, 커버 레터는 신청자가 희망하는 해당부서에 대한 관심과 자신의 자격을 설명하는 문서이다. 대부분의 회사는 이력서를 검토하기 전에 커버 레터를 읽는다.

Cover Letter Writing Tips 커버 레터 쓰기 팁

Writing an effective cover letter is as important as creating a good resume. Most employers do not spend a lot of time reading cover letters, so it is essential to personalize your cover letter to the needs of each job you are applying for. Without this kind of effort, it will be difficult to obtain an interview. For some companies, they use a computer software to select the most appropriate applicants to bring in for an interview. Thus, when the information in your cover letter aligns closer to the job description, you will have a higher chance to get selected for an interview.

Sample Chronological Resume
연대순 이력서 샘플

Hee Jung Chang
12345, Bangbaedong, Seocho-gu, Seoul, Korea
(H): 02-1234-5678   (C): 010-1234-5678
E-mail : chang000@naver.com

Objective

Professional and enthusiastic individual looking for a flight attendant position with _____. Highly motivated and customer-service oriented with 3+ years of service experience.

Education

_____ UNIVERSITY	Seoul, KR
Associate Degree in Airline Service	February 2018
Awarded Academic Scholarship	February 2017

Work Experience

PARADISE HOTEL	Seoul, KR
Front Desk Receptionist	May 2016 - July 2017

- Answered telephone calls and provided assistance to guests.
- Resolved guest complaints promptly.
- Assisted guests with 'over bookings' and 'booking changes'.
- Greeted and assisted local company representatives.
- Responded to questions on Facebook, Home Page, and Blog queries.
- Managed the reservation sites (booking.com/ expedia/ hotel.com) and the homepage.

FAMILY RESTAURANT	Seoul, KR
SERVER	August 2014 - April 2016

- Received orders and answered questions to the dishes on the menu.
- Served customers and helped customers select food and beverages.
- Took charge in the front counter and received payments.
- Collaborated with other restaurant staff and provided assistance in the kitchen.
- Distributed company fliers in the street to advertise the restaurant.

Additional Skills

- CRS(Computer reservation system) Topas Sell Connect & Abacus
- Bilingual in Chinese and English, Fluent in Korean

Reference available on request

효과적인 커버 레터를 작성하는 것은 좋은 이력서를 만드는 것만큼 중요하다. 대부분의 고용주는 커버 레터를 읽는데 많은 시간을 소비하지 않으므로 신청하는 각 직업의 필요에 맞게 커버 레터를 개인화하는 것이 필수적이다. 이런 노력이 없다면 인터뷰를 얻기가 어려울 것이다. 일부 회사의 경우 컴퓨터 소프트웨어를 사용하여 인터뷰를 위해 가장 적합한 지원자를 선택한다. 따라서 당신의 커버 레터에 있는 정보가 본인이 지원한 직업에 적합하다면, 면접에서 선정될 가능성이 높아진다.

Always use simple and clear language and proofread. Editing is very important to catch any errors. You might also want to ask a colleague or a professional in the similar industry to review your cover letter.

항상 간단하고 명확한 언어를 사용하고 제출하기 전에 교정해야 한다. 오류를 잡으려면 편집이 매우 중요하다. 비슷한 업계의 동료나 전문가에게 커버 레터를 검토 받도록 하라.

Necessary Elements in a Cover Letter 커버 레터에 필요한 요소

Include the following information when writing a cover letter:
커버 레터를 쓸 때 다음과 같은 내용을 포함하라.

Your Name and Contact Information 당신의 이름과 연락처 정보

Your name and contact information are written at the top of your cover letter. Your contact information should include first and last name, address, phone number, and email address.

당신의 이름과 연락처는 커버 레터의 상단에 쓰면 된다. 연락처 정보에는 이름, 성, 주소, 전화 번호 및 이메일 주소가 포함되어야한다.

Date 날짜

Include the date when you are writing the letter.
당신이 편지를 작성하는 날짜를 쓴다.

The Hiring Manager's Name and Contact Information

고용 담당자의 이름 및 연락처 정보

Include the following information: 다음과 같은 내용이 들어가도록 작성하라.

☑ The name of the hiring manager 고용 담당자의 이름

☑ The hiring manager's position and the name of his/her company
  고용 담당자의 직책과 회사명

☑ His/her contact information including address and phone number.
  고용 담당자의 주소와 전화번호

Salutation 인사말

Address to the hiring manager using his/her last name (i.e., Dear Mr. Smith). If you do not know the hiring manager's name, you can write, Dear Hiring Manager." That is better to use than the generic salutation, "To Whom It May Concern."

성을 사용하여 채용 담당자에게 지원하라 (예시, 친애하는 Mr. Smith). 고용 담당자의 이름을 모르는 경우 "고용 담당자께"라고 쓸 수 있다. 그것은 "대면 할 수 있는 사람에게" 라는 일반적인 인사말을 사용하는 것보다 더 좋다.

Introduction 서론

Start your introduction by stating the position you are applying for and where you found out about the job opportunity information. Briefly state how your educational background, skills, and/or experience match the position.

지원하고자 하는 직책과 취업 정보를 발견한 방법을 적고 소개를 시작하라. 당신의 교육 배경, 기술 및 / 또는 경험이 그 직책과 어떻게 일치하는지 간략하게 작성한다.

Details 본문

Review the job posting carefully. Mention relevant skills you possess that are specific to the position and explain why you are the right person for the job. Use specific examples from your previous job to explain how you can contribute to the company.

본인이 지원한 직업 공고를 신중하게 검토하라. 직책과 관련된 관련 기술을 언급하고 그 직무에 본인이 적합한 이유를 적는다. 어떻게 하면 회사에 기여할 수 있다는 것을 설명하기 위해 이전 직업의 구체적인 예를 사용하라.

Sample Cover Letter
커버 레터 샘플

Your Name
Home Address
Phone Number
Cell Number
Email Address

Date

Hiring Manager's First and Last Name
Hiring Manager's Title
Company Name
Company Address

Dear Mr./Ms. Last Name,

I have recently graduated from _____ University with an associate degree in airline service. As posted on _____airways.com, I am excited to know that there is an opening for a flight attendant position with your airline. I am enclosing my resume for your review, and I would like to be considered for the cabin crew position.

I believe I have the educational background and work experience that will be useful to work as a flight attendant. In college, I took many relevant courses such as global manners, airline ticketing and reservations, image making, and food and beverage service courses to help me work comfortably in the airline industry. In addition to taking many foreign language courses, I also took advantage of doing a study abroad program while in college. Because of the study abroad experience, I am proficient in Chinese as well as in English.

While in college I have held several service jobs. I have over two years of experience working at a wedding hall providing high quality service to brides and grooms as well as to their guests. I received high praises from my supervisor for my positive attitude and professional mannerism when working with customers. I also worked at a family restaurant and at a cafe gaining excellent customer service skills. As a result of my varied work experiences, I have gained effective service and teamwork skills. I believe these skills will be valuable when I work as a flight attendant.

I would welcome the opportunity to interview with you. I can be reached at 010-1000-2000 or via email at ooooo@email.com. Thank you for your consideration. I look forward to hearing from you soon!

Sincerely,

Your Name

Closing 마무리

In the closing section, restate how your skills align with the needs of the position and why you are interested in the position. Ask the hiring manager to review your resume and to be considered for the position. State how you can be contacted and provide your contact information.

종결 섹션에서는 본인이 지원하고자 하는 직책과 가지고 있는 기술이 어떻게 적합한지 다시 알려주어야 한다. 고용주에게 이력서를 검토하고 자신이 맡을 직책에 대해 고려하도록 요청 한다. 연락할 수 있는 방법을 기재하고 연락처 정보를 제공하라.

 Let's Practice English · 영어를 연습해 보자

Activity 1: Writing 쓰기

Creating A Resume 이력서 만들기

Before creating a resume, let's first brainstorm and prepare the process by gathering information about yourself.

이력서를 작성하기 전에 먼저 브레인스토밍을 하고 자신에 대한 정보를 수집하여 이력 서 작성과정을 준비하라.

In the first column, list the jobs you have held. You can also include major school activity or any volunteer experience.

첫 번째 칸에 보유한 직업을 적어라. 또한 주요 학교 활동이나 자원 봉사 경험을 포함 하라.

In the second column, describe using action verbs what you did in each job or activity.

두 번째 칸에는 행동 동사를 사용하여 각 직업이나 활동에서 어떤 일을 했는지 설명한다.

List the skills you have gained from your work, school, or volunteer experience in the third column.

세 번째 칼럼에서는 직장, 학교 또는 자원 봉사 경험을 통해 얻은 기술을 기재하라.

In the last column, include any awards or recognition you have received from your various experiences.

마지막 칸에는 다양한 경험을 통해 얻은 상훈이나 표창을 포함하라.

Sample 샘플

Job/ Work Experience	Duties/ Responsibilities	Skills	Rewards/ Achievements
List each job held or major school activity participated; or volunteer experience	Describe in action verbs what you did in each job or activity	List some of the relevant skills or abilities resulting from each job, activity, or volunteer experience	Indicate any kind of recognition/ award you received from your work, school, or volunteer experience
Hotel Receptionist	1) Answered telephone calls; 2) provided assistance to guests; 3) resolved guests complaints.	1) Communication skills; 2) follow through; 3) problem solving skills	Received praises from customers and supervisor
Food Server	1) Received orders; 2) answered questions about the dishes on the menu; 3) worked in the cash register	1) People skills; 2) professionalism; 3) high quality service skills	Customers expressed their gratitude
Administrative Assistant	1) Answered telephone calls; 2) responded to inquiries; 3) provided office support to staff and management	1) Organizational skills; 2) prioritizing skills; 3) ability to work in busy working environment	Received an offer of a permanent position
Sales Person	1) Provided service to customers; 2) ordered merchandise; 3) displayed products in the store	1) Customer skills; 2) communication skills; 3) problem solving skills	Performed 10% above sales goal

Include your information in the chart. 차트에 당신의 정보를 적어라.

Job/ Work Experience	Duties/ Responsibilities	Skills	Rewards/ Achievements
List each job held or major school activity participated; or volunteer experience	Describe in action verbs what you did in each job or activity	List some of the relevant skills or abilities resulting from each job, activity, or volunteer experience	Indicate any kind of recognition/ award you received from your work, school, or volunteer experience

Activity 2: Writing 쓰기

Writing A Cover Letter 커버 레터 작성하기

Let's practice writing a cover letter. Read the questions in each section below and write appropriate responses.

커버 레터를 작성하는 연습을 하자. 아래 각 섹션의 질문을 읽고 적절한 답변을 작성하라.

Your Name and Contact Information
당신의 이름과 연락처 정보

☑ Your first and last name, address, phone number, and email address

Date 날짜

☑ The date when you are writing the letter

The Hiring Manager's Name and Contact Information
고용 관리자의 이름 및 연락처 정보

☑ The name of the hiring manager you're writing to

☑ The hiring manager's position or the name of his/her company

☑ His/her contact information including address and phone number

Salutation 인사말

Dear Mr./Ms. _____,

Introduction 서론

☑ What position are you applying for?
  어떤 직책을 신청합니까?

☑ Where did you find out about the job opportunity information?

　어디서 일자리 정보를 찾았습니까?

☑ How do your educational background, skills, and/or experience match the position?

　당신의 교육 배경, 기술 및 / 또는 경험이 그 직책과 어떻게 일치합니까?

Details 본문

☑ What relevant skills do you possess that are specific to the position?

　해당 직책과 관련하여 보유하고 있는 관련 기술은 무엇입니까?

☑ Why are you the right person for the job?

　왜 당신이 이 직업에 가장 적합한 사람이라고 생각합니까?

☑ Please provide specific examples from your previous job to explain how you can contribute to the company.

　회사에 기여할 수 있다는 것을 설명하기 위해 이전 직업의 구체적인 예를 사용하라.

Closing 마무리

☑ How do your skills align with the needs of the position?

　당신의 기술은 그 직책의 필요에 어떻게 부합합니까?

☑ Why are you interested in the position?

　당신은 왜 이 직업에 관심이 있습니까?

☑ Ask the prospective employer to review your resume and to be considered for the position.

　고용주에게 이력서를 검토하고 자신이 맡을 직책에 대해 고려하도록 요청한다.

☑ State how you can be contacted and provide your contact information.

　연락할 수 있는 방법을 기재하고 연락처 정보를 제공하라.

Cover Letter Format

Your Name
Home Address
Phone Number/Cell Number
Email Address

Date

Hiring Manager's First and Last Name
Hiring Manager's Title
Company Name
Company Address

Dear Mr./Ms. _____,

지원하고자 하는 직책과 취업 정보를 발견한 방법을 적고 소개를 시작하라. 당신의 교육 배경, 기술 및 / 또는 경험이 그 직책과 어떻게 적합한지 간략하게 작성한다.

직책과 관련된 관련 기술을 언급하고 그 직무에 본인이 적합한 이유를 적는다. 회사에 기여할 수 있다는 것을 설명하기 위해 이전 직업의 구체적인 예를 사용하라.

종결 섹션에서는 본인이 지원하고자 하는 직책과 가지고 있는 기술이 어떻게 일치하는지 다시 알려주어야 한다. 고용주에게 이력서를 검토하고 자신이 맡을 직책에 대해 고려하도록 요청한다. 연락 할 수 있는 방법을 기재하고 연락처 정보를 제공하라.

Sincerely,

서명

First & Last Name

Appendices
부록

 Appendix 1: Comprehensive Chapter Vocabulary List
전체 단위 어휘 목록

☀ Chapter 3

maintain	improve	beneficial
similarities	aware of	socialize
practical	acquired	task
pertinent	inform	varied
develop	effective	coworkers

☀ Chapter 4

command	overcame	appreciate
enormous	conflict	maintain
sophisticated	consecutively	align

diversity	advancement	path
accomplish	reputable	assets
deadlines	consider	practical

☀ Chapter 5

ensure	in charge of	regardless
perform	unexpected	pride
irritable	professionalism	posses
combination	exceptional	committed
obtain	first-aid	achieve

☀ Chapter 6

previous	mediocre	blunt
suitable	require	task
diverse	priority	pride
encourage	appropriate	excel
specific	uptight	loosen up

☀ Chapter 7

| resolve | conflicts | identify |
| reflect | perspective | manner |

suffered	attentively	inform
fault	frustration	remedy
unexpected	relate	discuss

☀ Chapter 8

refuse	consequence	remind
monitor	surrounding	demand
attentive	intoxicated	option
rude	mishap	proactive
fine	allow	instead
complimentary	laundry	incident

☀ Chapter 9

reputable	mannerism	ultimate
launch	competitive	destination
initially	established	promptly
possess	carrier	impressed
exceptional	sophisticated	interact

Appendix 2: Comprehensive Chapter Interview Question List 전체 단위 인터뷰 질문 목록

⁂ Chapter 1

Q.1 Is your name _____? Can I have your name and number, please?

당신의 이름은 _____입니까?

당신의 이름과 응시 번호를 알려줄 수 있을까요?

Q.2 How are you today? How are you feeling today?

오늘 기분이 어떠세요?

Q.3 Where are you from?

어느 나라 사람인가요?

Q.4 Did you have any difficulty finding this place?

이 장소를 찾는데 어려움이 있었습니까?

Q.5 Where do you currently live?

지금 사는 곳이 어디입니까?

Q.6 How do you maintain good health?

건강관리를 어떻게 하시나요?

Q.7 What is your current job?

현재 무슨 일을 하나요?

Q.8 Have you applied for _____ Airline before?

전에 _____ 항공을 신청하셨습니까?

Q.9 What do you know about our airline?

우리 항공사에 대해 무엇을 아십니까?

Q.10 Is your phone number _____? Could we call you later today for the next assessment process?

전화번호는 _____입니까? 다음 평가 절차를 위해 오늘 늦게 전화 할 수 있습니까?

☀ Chapter 3

Q.1 Would you please tell me about yourself?

당신에 대해서 말해 주시겠습니까?

Q.2 Tell me about yourself.

당신에 대해 말해주세요.

Q.3 Can you introduce yourself?

당신 소개 좀 해줄래요?

Q.4 Could you tell us about yourself?

당신에 대해서 말해 주시겠습니까?

Q.5 What don't you tell us about yourself?

당신에 대해 우리에게 말해 주시겠습니까?

☀ Chapter 4

Q.1 Tell me briefly about yourself.

자신에 대하여 간단하게 말해 보세요.

Q.2 Why should we hire you?

왜 우리가 당신을 고용해야 하나요?

Q.3 Why do you want to work here?

당신은 왜 우리 회사에서 일하기를 원합니까?

Q.4 Where do you see yourself in five years?

당신은 5년 후 어떤 모습으로 있기를 원합니까?

Q.5 Do you have any questions for us?
우리에게 질문이 있습니까?

❈ Chapter 5

Q.1 What do you know about the duties of cabin crew members?
항공 승무원의 의무에 대해 무엇을 알고 있습니까?

Q.2 What are the important skills required by cabin crew members?
항공 승무원에게 요구되는 중요한 기술은 무엇입니까?

Q.3 Why do you want to become a cabin crew?
왜 항공 승무원이 되기를 원합니까?

Q.4 What are some advantages and disadvantages of being a cabin crew?
승무원 직업의 장점과 단점은 무엇입니까?

Q.5 Does your personality suit the job of a cabin crew?
당신의 성격이 항공 승무원의 직업에 적절한가요?

❈ Chapter 6

Q.1 What is your greatest strength? What are your greatest strengths?
당신의 가장 큰 강점은 무엇입니까?

Q.2 Why are you the best person for the job? Why should we choose you for the job?
왜 당신이 이 직업에 가장 적합한 사람이라고 생각합니까? 이 직업에 왜 우리가 당신을 선택해야 합니까?

Q.3 What is your greatest weakness? What are your weaknesses?
당신의 가장 큰 약점은 무엇입니까?

Q.4 What would you want to change about your personality?
당신의 성격에 관해 무엇을 바꾸고 싶습니까?

Q.5 What motivates you in life?
무엇이 당신의 삶에 동기를 부여합니까?

☀ Chapter 7

Q.1 How would you resolve conflicts in the workplace?
직장에서 갈등을 어떻게 해결할 것입니까?

Q.2 How would you handle an unsatisfied customer?
불만족을 느끼는 고객에게 어떻게 대처하십니까?

Q.3 Do you have any failure or disappointment in your life?
If so, what did you learn from the experience?

당신 인생에서 어떤 실패나 실망이 있었습니까?
그렇다면 그 경험에서 무엇을 배웠습니까?

Q.4 Describe a difficult work situation you have had and tell me how you handled it.

어려운 업무상황에 대해 설명하고 대처하는 방법을 알려주십시오.

Q.5 How do you handle stress?
스트레스를 어떻게 해소하십니까?

☀ Chapter 8

Q.1 How would you deal with a passenger who refuses to fasten the seatbelt?

안전벨트 착용을 거부하는 승객을 어떻게 대응하겠습니까?

Q.2 How would you deal with a drunken passenger who keeps asking for more alcohol?

만취한 승객이 계속해서 알코올을 원한다면 당신은 어떻게 대응하겠습니까?

Q.3 How would you deal with a demanding and rude passenger?

당신은 까다롭고 무례한 승객을 어떻게 대응하겠습니까?

Q.4 What would you do if there was a passenger smoking in the lavatory?

만약 승객이 화장실에서 흡연을 한다면 어떻게 하겠습니까?

Q.5 What would you do if you spilled juice or water to a passenger due to a sudden turbulence?

만약 갑작스러운 기류 변화로 인해 주스나 물을 승객에게 엎질렀다면 어떻게 하겠습니까?

⁂ Chapter 9

Q.1 Why do you want to work for this airline (company)?

왜 이 항공사 (회사) 에서 일하기를 원하십니까?

Q.2 Who are the major competitors of this airline (company)?

이 항공사 (회사)의 주요 경쟁자는 누구입니까?

Q.3 What do you know about our airline (company)?

우리 항공사 (회사)에 대해 무엇을 아십니까?

Q.4 How has your education/experience prepared you for your career?

당신의 교육 / 경험은 당신의 경력을 위해 어떻게 준비해 왔습니까?

Q.5 What can you contribute to this company?

이 회사에 당신은 무엇을 기여하겠습니까?

Appendix 3: Action Verbs for Resume Writing
이력서 작성을 위한 행동 동사

People/Service Skills	Teamwork Skills	Leadership Skills
advised	cooperated	coordinated
supported/advocated	directed	led
served	facilitated	executed
informed	fostered	headed
guided	mentored	operated
resolved	motivated	developed
enhanced	coached	implemented
handled	promoted	introduced
managed	persuaded	created
achieved	inspired	built
solved	guided	designed
improved	strengthened	oversaw
provided	taught	planned
generated	trained	produced
maximized	influenced	organized
developed	achieved	supervised

boosted	expedited	managed
advanced	generated	delegated
modified	maximized	discovered
transformed	delivered	controlled
delivered	boosted	formulated
addressed	advanced	initiated
arranged	modified	directed
communicated	transformed	enforced
hosted	collaborated	established
responded	discussed	administered
participated	presented	assigned
involved	interacted	executed
consulted	distributed	attained
explained	conducted	chaired
interacted	encouraged	approved
promoted	informed	eliminated
presented	stimulated	prioritized
assisted	organized	recommended
ushered	gathered	supervised
cared for	proposed	instructed

contributed	identified	reorganized
answered	convinced	restored
encouraged	advocated/supported	reinforced
supplied	simplified	recruited
aided	supplied	proposed
resolved	adapted	performed
volunteered	determined	proposed

Appendix 4: Sample Cabin Crew Interview Questions
항공사 기출 문제

※ Personal/Family Related Questions
개인 신상/가족에 관한 질문

Q1. Do PR for yourself.

Q2. How do you handle stress?

Q3. How is your personality?

Q4. What is your greatest strength?

Q5. What is your weakness?

Q6. Tell me about your family.

Q7. What do your parents think of you becoming a flight attendant?

Q8. What is your hobby?

Q9. How do you spend your free time?

Q10. Do you have overseas experience?

Q11. Have you ever felt disappointment in your life or at work?

Q12. What was the biggest challenge in your life?
     How did you overcome it?

Q13. How did you prepare yourself to be a cabin crew?

Q14. What are you most proud of?

Q15. Who do you respect the most? Why?

❋ Questions Related To School/Major
학교/전공에 관한 질문

Q1. What is your major?

Q2. Why did you choose your major?

Q3. Are you satisfied with your major?

Q4. Do you have school club experience?

Q5. What did you learn from your school club experience?

Q6. What did you like about your college life?

Q7. Tell me about your major.

Q8. What was the biggest challenge while attending college?

Q9. Did you work while in college?

Q10. What do you remember the most about your college life?

Q11. Do you have any regrets?

Q12. What was your favorite course?

Q13. What kind of student were you?

Q14. What other foreign languages do you speak?

Q15. What was your least favorite course?

☀ Service Related Questions
서비스 관한 질문

Q1. What does good service look like to you?

Q2. Tell me when you provided the best service to a customer.

Q3. What is your own definition of good service?

Q4. What is important in providing good service?

Q5. Did you ever handle an unhappy customer? How did you handle the customer?

Q6. Have you had a customer who asked a difficult request?

Q7. Tell me about the time when you received the top quality service.

Q8. Describe a difficult customer. How would you handle the customer?

Q9. What is more important, service or safety?

Q10. Tell me about the time when you received poor service. How did you handle the situation?

❋ Questions Related to Work Experience
직장/경력에 관한 질문

Q1. Tell me about your work experience.

Q2. How did your work experience prepare you for this position?

Q3. What was the most challenging moment while working?

Q4. Do you think you are qualified for this job?

Q5. What was the most memorable moment from your previous job?

Q6. Does your work experience match the needs of this position?

Q7. Do you prefer working alone or on a team?

Q8. Have you ever had a conflict with your coworker? How did you handle the situation?

Q9. How would your previous coworkers (supervisors) describe you?

Q10. What do you think of multitasking?

Q11. What has been the biggest accomplishment in your career?

Q12. What motivates you?

Q13. How do you handle stress?

Q14. What would you bring to this company?

Q15. If your coworker constantly does not do his/her job, how will you handle the situation?

☀ Questions Related to Study Abroad or Overseas Experience
해외경험 및 연수경험에 관한 질문

Q1. Do you have any overseas experience?

Q2. Have you ever been abroad for studying English?

Q3. Do you like traveling?

Q4. What was the most memorable moment of your overseas trip?

Q5. Have you felt any cultural difference when you stayed in a foreign country?

Q6. Was there a difficult moment while you were abroad?

Q7. Which country do you wish to visit the most when you become a flight attendant?

Q8. What did you learn from your overseas trip?

Q9. Have you ever felt culture shock while studying abroad?

Q10. What did you miss most about Korea while traveling?

Q11. Do you think studying abroad is necessary to learn a foreign language?

Q12. Tell me positive points about studying abroad.

Q13. What advice would you offer to a student who is thinking about studying abroad?

Q14. What countries have you visited?

Q15. What was your favorite country and why?

☀ Airline Related Questions
항공사 관련 질문

Q1. What do you know about our airline?

Q2. What image comes to your mind when you think of our company?

Q3. Have you used our airline? How would you rate our service?

Q4. Why do you want to join our airline?

Q5. What have you prepared to work for our airline?

Q6. What characteristics are important for _____ flight attendants?

Q7. Have you reviewed our company's website? What do you think of it?

Q8. What recent news have you heard about our airline?

Q9. What do you think of our uniform?

Q10. What would you gain from working at our company?

Q11. What do you know about the duties of flight attendants?

Q12. This position requires a lot of traveling. How will you manage it?

Q13. What are some advantages/disadvantages of becoming a cabin crew?

Q14. What are the three major qualifications needed to become a cabin crew?

Q15. Why do you want to become a flight attendant?

✳ Questions Related To Resume
이력서 관련된 질문

Q1.   Please tell me about yourself.

Q2.   Can you walk me through your resume?

Q3.   What did you study in college? Why did you choose the major?

Q4.   Tell me about your job experience.

Q5.   Describe the responsibilities or duties in your last position.

Q6.   What skills have you gained from working at _____ ?

Q7.   What are you most proud of?

Q8.   What are your professional or career goals?

Q9.   Tell me about your volunteer experience.

Q10. What were some challenges from your previous job?

Appendix 5: Important Vocabulary for Foreign Airline Interview & Recruitment Process
외국항공사 인터뷰 및 모집 프로세스를 위한 중요한 어휘

- ☑ Excellent Health & Fitness 우수한 건강 및 피트니스
- ☑ Arm Reach Check 팔 도달 길이
- ☑ Minimum Height Requirement 최소 신장 요구 사항
- ☑ Formal Business Attire 공식 비즈니스 복장
- ☑ Open Day 오픈데이
- ☑ English Assessment 영어 평가
- ☑ Pre-employment medical assessment 취업 전 의료 평가
- ☑ Resume/Curriculum Vitae (CV) 이력서
- ☑ Cover Letter 커버 레터
- ☑ Highest Education Certificate/Diploma 최종 학위 증명서/졸업 증서
- ☑ Original 원본
- ☑ Passport Photocopy 여권 사본
- ☑ Dress Code 복장 요구
- ☑ Demonstrate 증명하다
- ☑ Identity Card 신분증

Appendix 6: Airlines & Website Homepage Information
항공사 및 항공사 웹 사이트 홈페이지 정보

Visit the following airlines' website homepages to learn more about their recruitment requirements and hiring processes.

채용 정보 및 채용 프로세스에 대한 자세한 내용을 보려면 다음 항공사의 웹 사이트 홈페이지를 방문하라.

⭐ Korean Air (대한 항공)

https://recruit.koreanair.co.kr/

⭐ Asiana Airline (아시아나 항공)

https://recruit.flyasiana.com/

⭐ Jeju Air (제주항공)

http://recruit.jejuair.net/main.jsp

⭐ Jin Air (진에어)

http://jinair.career.co.kr/

⭐ Air Busan (에어부산)

https://recruit.airbusan.com/

⭐ T'Way (티웨이항공)

https://recruit.twayair.com/WiseRecruitWeb/

⭐ Emirates Airline (에미레이트 항공)

http://www.emiratesgroupcareers.com/cabin-crew/

⭐ Qatar Airways (카타르항공)

http://careers.qatarairways.com/qatarairways/vacancysearch.aspx

⭐ Cathay Pacific (캐세이퍼시픽 항공)

https://jobs.cathaypacific.com/

⭐ Singapore Airlines (싱가포르 항공)

http://www.singaporeair.com/ko_KR/kr/careers/

⭐ Philippines Air (필리핀 항공)

https://www.philippineairlines.com/en/kr/home

⭐ China Eastern Air (중국 동방 항공)

http://www.easternair.co.kr/

⭐ China Southern Airlines (중국 남방 항공)

http://cs-air.co.kr/

⭐ Air China (중국 국제 항공)

https://www.airchina.kr/

⭐ Cathay Dragon Air (캐세이 드레곤 에어)

https://www.cathaypacific.com/cx/ko_KR.html

⭐ Air Macau (에어마카오)

http://www.airmacau.co.kr/web/home/home_list.asp

⭐ Finn Air(핀에어)

https://www.finnair.com/kr/ko/

⭐ Air France (에어 프랑스)

http://www.airfrance.co.kr/

⭐ Garuda Indonesia (가루다 인도네시아 항공)

https://www.garuda-indonesia.com/kr/ko/index.page

⭐ Etihad Airways (에티하드 항공)

http://www.etihad.com/ko-kr/

⭐ KLM Royal Dutch Airlines (KLM 네덜란드 항공)

https://www.klm.com/

⭐ Lufthansa (루프트한자 독일항공)

http://www.lufthansa.com/kr/ko/Homepage

⭐ Malaysia Airlines (말레이시아 항공)

https://www.malaysiaairlines.com/kr/en.html

⭐ All Nippon Airways, ANA (ANA 항공)

http://www.ana.co.jp/asw/wws/kr/k/

⭐ Thai Airways (타이항공)

http://www.thaiairways.com/ko_KR/index.page

⭐ Vietnam Airlines (베트남 항공)

https://www.vietnamairlines.com/ko/home

⭐ Hainan Airlines (중국 하이난 항공)

http://www.hnair.com/

References

Dos and Don'ts of GD, Group Discussion. (n.d.)
    Retrieved from
        http://www.careerride.com/Group-Discussion-dos-dont.aspx

Doyle, A. (2017, July 28). Top 10 Job Interview Tips. Retrieved from
        https://www.thebalance.com/top-job-interview-tips-2061331

Doyle, A. (2018, February, 21). Cover Letter Examples and Writing Tips.
        Retrieved from https://www.thebalance.com

Doyle, A. (2017, July 14). Resume Types: Chronological, Functional, Combination.
        Retrieved from https://www.thebalance.com

Flight Attendant Requirements in 2017. (n.d.).
    Retrieved from
        http://www.careerflightpath.com/flight-attendant-requirements/

Lee, J. (2017). *English Interview for Cabin Crew: Mastering English
    Interviewing Skills*. Hanol Publishing Company.

Murphy, R. (2009). *Grammar in Use Intermediate*. Cambridge University
    Press.

Open & Assessment Day - Qatar Airways Cabin Crew/Flight Attendant
    Interview Day Review. Retrieved from
        https://www.youtube.com/watch?v=Eg77NemzWiQ

저자 소개

| 이제시카선규 |

학력

- University of Colorado at Boulder 경영학과 졸업
- University of Colorado at Dever 교육대학원 교육학석사
- George Washington University 교육대학원 교육학박사

- 현) 백석예술대학교 항공서비스과 교수
- 전) George Washington University 이중 언어 특수교육 프로그램 방문 교수
- Office of English Language Acquisition – US Department of Education 에서 지원하는 Bridges to Curriculum Access 프로그램 연구 과학자

Success in English Interview for Cabin Crew:
How to Win the Job Interview

**항공 승무원을 위한 성공 영어 인터뷰:
면접에서 승리하는 방법**

초판1쇄 발행   2018년 3월 10일
2판1쇄 발행   2019년 2월 20일

저   자 이제시카선규
펴 낸 이 임 순 재
펴 낸 곳 (주)한올출판사
등   록 제11-403호
주   소 서울시 마포구 모래내로 83(성산동, 한올빌딩 3층)
전   화 (02)376-4298(대표)
팩   스 (02)302-8073
홈 페 이 지 www.hanol.co.kr
e – 메 일 hanol@hanol.co.kr
I S B N 979-11-5685-750-1